Policy Matters:
EDUCATING CONGRESS ON PEACE AND SECURITY

Lorelei Kelly and Elizabeth Turpen, Ph.D.

Cover design by Design Army.

ISNB 0-9747255-7-9

The Henry L. Stimson Center
11 Dupont Circle, NW   Ninth Floor   Washington, DC 20036
phone 202.223.5956   fax 202.238.9604
www.stimson.org

Table of Contents

Chapter Six

Putting Together the Pieces: The Story of Security for a New

Foreword

I am pleased to present this new publication by the *Security for a New Century* project of the Henry L. Stimson Center. **Policy Matters: Educating Congress on Peace and Security** is intended to serve as a practical guide for individuals, groups and organizations that seek to engage Members of Congress on critical issues affecting America's role in the world, and on a wide array of national security policies and programs. It is intended to help citizens work with Congress to identify and develop shared understanding about national and international security. The "education" part of this book is really a two-way street: to help Members of Congress develop positions on key issues, citizens must be better educated and savvy in how Congress works. They need to learn about what techniques are effective in getting the attention of busy lawmakers, how committees work, and what communications strategies are likely to achieve desired results. All these issues are addressed in this useful book.

The Stimson Center is proud to sponsor the *Security for New Century* project, which provides congressional staff a continual series of briefings on a very diverse range of security-related issues. This program is intended to help all congressional staff, and it enjoys bipartisan support. The briefings are informational and do not advocate specific legislative solutions to the many problems and challenges in promoting peace and security. Its co-directors, Lorelei Kelly and Elizabeth Turpen, bring a wealth of practical and academic experience and knowledge to the program, and are the co-authors of this new publication.

I'll welcome hearing from you if you have any questions or comments.

Ellen Laipson
President and CEO
The Henry L. Stimson Center

Acknowledgments

We are exceedingly grateful to our supporters for making this publication possible. Their enthusiasm and commitment not only provided the impetus for this book, but has also enabled us to help educate Congress through the *Security for a New Century* program. Our funders include the Carnegie Corporation of New York, John D. and Catherine T. MacArthur Foundation, Ploughshares Fund, Prospect Hill Foundation, Rockefeller Brothers Fund, Scherman Foundation, and United States Institute of Peace.

We are grateful to our thoughtful reviewers who read our initial drafts and offered hard-hitting and helpful critiques that greatly enhanced this final product. Our heartfelt thanks go to Kathy Gille, Kate Turner, Sarah Devine, Kim Abbott, Susannah Cernojevich, Lee Ross, Sean Meyer, Stanton Denman, Alton Frye, Jim Dykstra, and Tim Mooney. Our friends in uniform, LTC Richard Lacquement and LTC Tony Pfaff also read drafts and helped sharpen our understanding of grand strategy and military issues.

We would also like to take this opportunity to thank individuals who have been vital to the success of *Security for a New Century* through their unflagging encouragement and creative spirit. They include Elizabeth Furse, Lynn Woolsey, Amy Butler, Chris Seiple, Bill Tate, and Erin Sheerin. Special thanks go to all the folks at the Stanford Center on Conflict and Negotiation as well as Steve Toben—an individual to whom the entire field of conflict resolution owes a great deal.

Most importantly, this publication would not have been possible without the insightful and good-humored collaboration and support of Adam J. Hantman. We are also grateful to Michael Heller, Nate Olson, Elizabeth Blumenthal, and other Stimson staff who helped bring this project to fruition.

Finally, we would also like to express our appreciation to all our generous colleagues and friends from non-governmental organizations, on Capitol Hill, in the US military, and at academic institutions for their interest and suggestions in our publication of this work. Their conviction that institutions and everyday citizens would benefit from the lessons of the *Security for a New Century* project provided the inspiration to write this book. We hope our efforts meet their expectations.

Lorelei Kelly and Elizabeth Turpen
Co-Directors, *Security for a New Century*

Introduction

If you think the United States has not adequately adapted its post-Cold War and post-September 11th strategy and institutions for effective engagement with the world, this handbook can serve as a tool to help you in your efforts to communicate with Members of Congress. If you believe, as we do, that Congress needs to focus more effort on preventive peace-building, provide more money for diplomatic solutions and less for Cold War-era weapons systems, ensure that capabilities for "winning the peace" match the US wherewithal to prevail in combat—if you believe, in general, that Congress frequently fails to pursue innovative, long-term solutions to today's peace and security challenges—then we hope that these pages will help you better understand the ins, outs, and peculiarities of Congress. We hope ultimately to assist you in formulating an effective strategy for getting your voice heard.

The audience we hope to reach is diverse and broadly distributed across a range of peace and security issues. This book might, for instance, be helpful to: an immigrant rights organization with creative ideas to help address the problem of human trafficking; a computer scientist who wants to make available her expertise on issues of networked threats; a student of conflict resolution who seeks to share knowledge about the art and science of peacemaking; a doctor who hopes to promote preventive measures to transnational health threats; a church group that would like to expand its efforts in poverty reduction; or teachers who seek to create a library program for secular education in South Asia. The possibilities for involvement in peace and security activities are not only abundant; they also change and evolve constantly.

We believe that with some thoughtful planning, the argument that cooperative engagement—from military alliances, to sister-cities programs, to faith-based humanitarian initiatives—is an important component in addressing today's challenges that can be propelled to the "radar screen" of Congress. But the people with the means of translating this argument into an explicit policy action, especially those with practical, "on-the-ground" experience, will need a solid strategy for bringing their proposals to the attention of policymakers. The collective objective of such individual strategies should be to promote an appropriate set of policies—and the corresponding tools—to address global challenges. In order to accomplish our goals, we must offer our knowledge to a Capitol Hill audience, organize to ensure sufficient attention is paid to long-term goals, and help to translate the American public's values into priorities for elected leaders. Above all, we view this as an exchange—a long-term dialogue between the public and its elected leaders. Listening and learning must happen on both sides.

We write this from a common premise: In today's post-September 11th world, our nation must move beyond the notion that military dominance is sufficient to prevail against threats to peace and security. We hope to inform and support Americans who would like their elected leadership to use all instruments of power at our nation's disposal so that force is truly only used as an instrument of last resort. Our objective is to achieve that by providing a user-friendly "how-to" manual that sheds light on the institutional tendencies and limitations of the US Congress, and offers tips on how to navigate them.

Chapter 1 offers a brief background on US global engagement and American attitudes on the US role in the world. If a majority of Americans believe that cooperative international engagement is important, then why doesn't Congress devote more time and resources to promote it? Chapter 1 briefly discusses our assumptions, the gap between polls and policymakers' beliefs about public opinion, and why Congress is a good place to start promoting change.

Chapter 2 looks at congressional institutions in the context of a post-Cold War and post-September 11th world. Why is Congress so rigidly attached to old-fashioned ways of doing business and setting priorities? Why do "hard" power solutions (e.g., weapons and technology) appear to have an overwhelming advantage over "soft" power solutions like preventive strategies for weak states or US efforts to secure nuclear weapons materials at the source? What drives the congressional agenda, and what can an engaged constituency do to influence it? What has or has not changed in Congress to ensure the institution's capability to adequately understand and address today's peace and security issues? This chapter is a primer on how to think about Congress in context.

In Chapter 3, we explain the institutional and procedural parameters within which Members of Congress operate. How does the House differ from the Senate with respect to a Member's ability to champion an issue? How should a Member's party affiliation, committee assignments, seniority, and personal experience factor into an assessment of her potential wherewithal to provide leadership on your issue? Could you or your organization become the primary constituent advisor on a key peace and security issue? What role can the media play in getting the Member's attention and building your coalition? Using two case studies, Chapter 3 walks you through the different factors that constrain or enhance a Member's potential leadership and the various roles Members play, as well as, the symbiotic relationship between Members and the media. Our objective is to train you to think like a Member and formulate a strategy that helps the Member help you.

In Chapter 4, we discuss how information on an issue can be turned into useful knowledge for a Member of Congress and his staff. What recommendations or "action items" are most relevant for Congress? Who is your audience and which committees (or Members) should you approach? What are successful tactics for getting access to your targeted Members? How can you frame an issue to avoid opposition, or provide as much common ground for support as possible? Again using two case studies, we escort you through the relevant committees and other potential audiences. We discuss strategies for getting access to Members' offices, and the value of online research tools to facilitate your search for potential allies. Finally, Chapter 4 outlines how to "package" your issues by paying attention to framing, partisan divisions, and terminology.

Chapter 5 is a primer on the "nuts and bolts" of Congress, including a brief summary of the legislative and budget process, tips on meetings with Members (or staffers), organizing public meetings on and off the Hill, methods for outreach, and logistics for obtaining a meeting room on Capitol Hill. What should you know about the legislative and budget process? What are important research and preparation tasks to ensure your event is topical, relevant, and framed in a way acceptable to a Member? How do you arrange a meeting in your district or on the Hill? What materials should you take along with you to the meeting? How might you set up an educational briefing on the Hill and appeal to a broad audience? We make recommendations for your planned office meetings and other, more advocacy-oriented peace and security events; in both cases, we discuss how to encourage your Member to participate. We then offer tips on controlling the agenda, on selecting your venue, and on the pros and cons of building a large coalition and co-hosting events.

Chapter 6 tells the story of *Security for a New Century* (*SNC*), an existing educational program on Capitol Hill and a major impetus for this publication. *SNC* is a bipartisan study group for congressional staffers. It meets regularly to discuss today's security challenges with US and international policy professionals. With its origins in conflict resolution theory developed at the Stanford Center on Conflict and Negotiation, this study group is an example of putting theory into practice. The creators of *SNC* posed and tried to address the following questions: How might we broaden the international outlook on Capitol Hill in the interest of the public good? How can we control for potential bias? What can be done to exclude power dynamics and partisan antagonism? We conclude this chapter with an analysis of why the program is successful and how it offers a model that others may wish to replicate.

A Little Bit of Background

— "When prevention succeeds, nothing happens."

— "International cooperation is just not sexy."

These are just two of the more telling lines we have heard during our years of work on foreign policy and defense issues in the US Congress. Such statements reveal the challenge put before those who would like to see Congress—largely stuck in Cold War thinking—broaden its international outlook and change its priorities to better reflect our post-September 11th world. There should be no doubt that sustained interest in international issues has always been a tough sell on Capitol Hill. It is our belief, however, that we now have an opportunity to change this reality, because both Americans and their elected leaders are paying more attention to issues outside US borders. But if Congress is reactive, how does the interested public generate congressional support for prevention? Can those who are committed formulate a strategy that makes conflict prevention and international cooperation more compelling?

Although it may not seem attentive (much less responsive), Congress functions as a two-way street between citizens and their elected representatives. While most Americans never interact with Congress on any issue, all of us are affected, indirectly or directly, by its policies. At the same time, Congress responds to the demands of constituents. Thus, it stands to reason that those who are most visible and best organized in their demands get more of what they want.

In this context, the question remains: How do those Americans who care about international cooperation and non-hardware defense issues ensure that their desires are reflected in the policy decisions and voting behaviors of their elected leaders?

We make some fundamental assumptions in this text. First and foremost, we assume that a domestic constituency for foreign policy exists. We also assume this constituency believes that the

United States has not adequately adapted either its institutions or thinking about today's peace and security concerns. Further, we argue that our elected leaders have not yet forged a consensus on what measures are appropriate to address today's challenges in a comprehensive, long-term, and cost-effective manner. Lastly, we assume that individuals share our assessment broadly across the political spectrum, although we recognize that everyone will not embrace these views.

Our assumption about a domestic constituency for active and cooperative US engagement is borne out by recent opinion polls. In poll after poll, the public supports active US engagement in the world. This was true before September 11th and remains so today. Research shows that Americans are not as isolationist, anti-United Nations (UN), or anti-foreign aid as is commonly thought. Polling data demonstrate that Americans do not approach foreign policy from a narrow what's-in-it-for-us self-interest, but from a deeply moral commitment to our national responsibility for maintaining world peace and well-being.[1] Polls also show significant support for the UN, especially when it is seen having a direct beneficial effect on American security. For instance, an overwhelming majority favors having the UN play a stronger role in the fight against terrorism, including in the strengthening of international laws on terrorism and the means to enforce them.[2]

It is also important to recognize the impact that public perceptions have on US engagement with the international community. In 2003, researchers concluded that Americans share a strong preference for cooperative international policies; however, Americans were also shown to underestimate public support for such policies and overestimate support for going it alone.[3] Yet polling and research about American attitudes on international

---

[1] Steven Kull and I.M. Destler, *Misreading the Public: The Myth of a New Isolationism* (Washington, DC: Brookings Institution Press, 1999). Or, more recently, Steven Kull's article "Voice of a Superpower," *Foreign Policy*, May/June 2004, p. 38.

[2] See, for instance, "Americans and the World: United Nations," *Program on International Policy Attitudes*; available online at www.americans-world.org/digest/global_issues/un/un_summary.cfm

[3] Alexander Todorov, "Public Opinion on Foreign Policy: The Multilateral Public that Perceives Itself as Unilateral," *Woodrow Wilson School of Public and International Affairs Policy Brief* (September 2003); available online at www.wws.princeton.edu/~policybriefs/todorov_opinion.pdf.

engagement highlight a significant challenge as well. As I.M. Destler points out, "The bad news is that general public support is not enough. On international engagement, Americans are permissive, not demanding."[4] In today's world, the public must begin making demands, if its majority views are to be heard frequently and forcefully enough to influence elected leaders.

As with many big-picture, long-term "common good" goals,[5] policy objectives like conflict prevention and cooperative security[6] do not mesh well with the short-term horizons of Capitol Hill, where two-, four-, and six-year election cycles take precedence. Most Members of the House and Senate, will, of course, claim to be in favor of international cooperation and will even agree about the need to view US security in its broadest sense. Their sentiments reflect a consistent majority of Americans who favor active US engagement and international cooperation.[7] With such a lofty goal in common, one would think that we would see farsighted and consistent actions on cooperative foreign policy programs more often. Yes, all too often, this is not the case.

---

[4] I.M.Destler, "The Reasonable Public and the Polarized Policy Process," in *The Real and the Ideal: Essays on International Relations in Honor of Richard H. Ullman*, eds. Anthony Lake and David Ochmanek (Lanham, Maryland: Rowman and Littlefield, 2001), p. 87.

[5] Examples of common goods might include "affordable and accessible healthcare, an effective system of public safety and security, peace among the nations of the world, a just legal and political system, an unpolluted natural environment and a flourishing economic system." (See "The Common Good," Markkula Center for Applied Ethics, Santa Clara University; available online at www.scu.edu/ ethics/practicing/decision/commongood.html).

[6] For our purposes, "cooperative security" connotes two or more countries voluntarily coordinating to address mutually identified threats. Activities under the US-Russia Cooperative Threat Reduction program to safely dismantle nuclear weapons and secure fissile materials constitute one example. The Bush Administration's Proliferation Security Initiative, under whose aegis states cooperate to enforce tighter export controls and interdict the transshipment of illicit goods, is another example.

[7] For a relevant sampling of statistics over the past several years, see "Americans on Terrorism: Two Years After 9/11," *Program on International Policy Attitudes* and *Knowledge Networks* (2003); "Worldviews 2002: American Public Opinion and Foreign Policy," Chicago Council on Foreign Relations (2002); "Americans on the War on Terrorism," *Program on International Policy Attitudes* (2001); and "American Public Opinion and US Foreign Policy 1999," Chicago Council on Foreign Relations (1999).

There is much work to be done by American citizens to promote US leadership in cooperative security if we are to successfully address today's many emerging security challenges. This work ranges from supporting Senate passage of international treaties beneficial to our long-term security interests, to encouraging representatives to look beyond their local pet projects. It will require an engaged public to find consensus on policy priorities and on the tools to address them. And it will demand a realistic strategy for conveying opinions about those priorities and tools to elected leaders and their staffs—the folks who make policy. The truth is that among policymakers and the public, when it comes to finding the right answers to modern security challenges, today's common denominator is uncertainty. What is therefore needed first is an acknowledgement of our shared uncertainty and a healthy discourse between the public and its elected leaders about the path forward.

Throughout our Capitol Hill experience working as staffers and directing a bipartisan educational study group on peace and security issues, we became aware of an acute need for more systematic knowledge-sharing between peace and security specialists and the policymakers in Congress. Staffers and Members have a huge appetite for credible, well-organized information on these issues. However, starting in the 1990s, and particularly following September 11th, the institution and its employees have experienced information overload, with no accompanying ability to interpret the available information and analysis. Due to time constraints and insufficient expertise, Congress now frequently lacks the internal capacity to process the information it receives. Our legislature has become a massive database in desperate need of a search engine.

Congress' need and appetite for knowledge, coupled with its constitutional role, makes it a good place to start with an educational strategy. Of the three branches of the federal government, Congress offers the most creative and diverse possibilities for individual citizens to effect change. At any one time, hundreds of bills are being crafted, introduced, negotiated, or debated. From the outside, Congress may seem at once omniscient and completely uncomprehending. After all, nearly every topic you can think of is considered at some point in the legislative process. Yet it often seems that important items are very hastily considered or completely overlooked. The good news is that there are many possible entry points for a dialogue with Congress on the benefits of cooperative security. Keep in mind that a focused strategy is crucial in order to contend with the time constraints of a fast-paced environment, some firmly entrenched institutional barriers, and the ever-present dynamics of turf battles and ego clashes.

Prior to addressing the development of a strategy, we must agree on some underlying concepts. Foreign policy has traditionally been the domain of the State Department. But with an increased blurring of the lines between domestic and international issues, more and more departments in the federal government are playing a role in US "foreign policy," understood in its broadest sense.[8] That said, when this handbook talks about foreign policy, we are generally referring to diplomatic, political, or economic means (i.e., the application of "soft" power) to achieve an objective or change another state's behavior.[9] When we discuss military means, or "hard" security, we are speaking about the use of force or coercion. At the same time, we fully recognize that since the end of the Cold War, the US military has been called upon for numerous Military Operations Other Than War ("MOOTW" in the Pentagon's own lexicon),[10] from peacekeeping in the Balkans to disaster response in Central America to counterterrorism deployments in the Republic of Georgia and the Philippines.

---

[8] A byproduct of globalization, the growing linkage of domestic and foreign affairs has led to formidable challenges in the management of US foreign policy. For a detailed discussion of these challenges and their implications, see Princeton N. Lyman, "Growing Influence of Domestic Factors," in *Multilateralism and US Foreign Policy,* eds. Stewart Patrick and Shepard Forman (Boulder: Lynne Rienner Publishers, 2002), pp. 75-97.

[9] Soft power is the ability to get what we want by attracting others, rather than by threatening or paying them. Soft power is based on our culture, our political ideals, and our policies. Joseph S. Nye is the originator of the terms "hard" and "soft" power. See, for example, Joseph S. Nye, "A Dollop of Deeper American Values: Why Soft Power Matters in Fighting Terrorism," *Washington Post,* Tuesday, March 30, 2004, Page A19.

[10] See "Overview of MOOTW" on the Defense Department's Joint Electronic Library www.dtic.mil/doctrine/jrm/mootw.doc. Military educational facilities offer a vast array of resources online. See, for example: www.ndu.edu or www.carlisle.army.mil.

We must also carefully distinguish between "national security," "foreign policy," and "defense." Defense and foreign policy are both subsets of national security. While our Department of Defense (i.e., the military) is the most visible symbol, US military means is only one element of our defense and foreign policy.[11] In its traditional role, the military's mission is to fight and win our nation's wars when all other measures to avert war have failed. The military's warfighting capacity also represents a psychological lever within our foreign policy "toolkit"; the threat of force provides necessary backing for other foreign policy measures (diplomatic, economic, etc.) utilized to bring about a desired outcome. Just as more federal agencies than in the past now play a role in US "foreign policy," multiple agencies (intelligence, homeland security, commerce, agriculture, health and human services, etc.) and actors (international and regional organizations, non-government organizations, and the private sector) will have to be involved in developing and implementing viable long-term solutions to today's challenges. Tremendous array of military and civilian tools are needed to achieve sustainable, long-term national security objectives. This array of tools—from hard to soft instruments of power—constitutes our nation's toolkit for addressing national security challenges and should be structured to function as an integrated whole.

In order for US national security policy to be informed, well reasoned, and effective, policymakers must both understand the possible components of a well-stocked toolkit and appreciate their uses. The purpose of this handbook is to lay out some new ways of thinking about today's security needs, and to suggest organizing strategies for local constituents so that, in the end, our elected leaders will better represent a full spectrum of policy options to achieve long-term peace and security.

This handbook focuses solely on the formulation of short-term, tactical strategies for citizens to engage with Members of Congress about their vision of the appropriate tools needed to address current security challenges. Two interrelated themes are threaded throughout the discussion of formulating a tactical strategy: one

---

[11] Even within the category of "defense," the means of the Pentagon can be broken down between the weapons and technology (commonly referred to as "hardware") for war-fighting on the one hand and the human capacities of our military services (referred to here as "non-hardware defense") on the other.

regarding process and the other regarding content. While the former requires, for example, navigating committee structures that do not match up well with post-Cold War threats, the latter addresses framing the content so that the link to US security interests is explicit.

Without question, addressing the "process problem" will require significant procedural and organizational changes in both Congress and within the national security apparatus of the executive branch.[12] We welcome the energy and commitment of those who share our concerns in shaping and implementing a long-term strategy for change. In the meantime, however, national and international challenges abound. Concerned citizens must navigate the institutions in their current form and help bridge the gap for policymakers regarding the relevance of non-military means in addressing today's security needs.

---

[12] For example, a re-write of the 1947 National Security Act may be appropriate to address a radically changed international environment. Such a re-write could address the need for an interagency military and civilian "surge" capacity to address post-conflict or peacekeeping needs, more coherence among agencies to achieve US nonproliferation objectives, greater institutional capacities to prevent state failure, or more effective means to conduct US public diplomacy.

Today's Congress in Context

While the world continues to change at a breathtaking pace, the structures, priorities, and processes of Capitol Hill remain outmoded and unyielding. Congress can seem trapped by traditional, structural, and procedural constraints that make rapid adaptation to a changed and changing world very difficult. These constraints on the ability and willingness to adapt are most acute in the realm of foreign and defense policy. Nonetheless, both the willingness to adapt and the guidance on the direction of change can come about through the active participation of an informed constituency.

This chapter offers an assessment of the missing ingredients on Capitol Hill required for consistent positive action on major global challenges and to ensure that our foreign policy toolkit[1] is well stocked and balanced. Although most elected leaders clearly value a peaceful and prosperous international environment, the measures taken to achieve this end are filtered through inflexible Cold War institutions in the federal government and, more specifically for our purposes, in Congress. As a result, the end product is often heavily weighted toward military solutions.

WHAT DRIVES THE AGENDA?

The agenda in this context is not only what gets debated on the floor of the House or Senate, but the dynamics internal to the committees and personal offices on Capitol Hill. From one day to the next the congressional agenda may shift, whether due to a scandal, a natural disaster, or any number of events that precipitate

---

[1] The spectrum of challenges ranges from weapons of mass destruction in the hands of terrorists and rogue states to global climate change. The US requires an effective strategy to rank priorities among the threats and opportunities and a way to gauge the most efficient means to address the threats or exploit possible opportunities. A comprehensive ranking of priorities and corresponding allocation of resources toward the means to address them is not currently taking place.

widespread public awareness and a corresponding expectation that our elected leaders should "fix" the problem. But unforeseen anomalies aside, some generalizations can be made with respect to the daily pressures that guide policymakers' decisions to commit time and effort to an issue. What drives the political agenda, and how can we affect these driving forces?

An item gets on the congressional agenda if sufficient political will exists to make it a priority. A politician may value a peaceful world and give lip service to a bountiful life for all humanity, but her values and wishes may not bear fruit unless they are given priority, and are not subsumed by interests that run counter to these objectives. An engaged constituency in support of these values can help create the political will and make the achievement of these ideals a priority. Further, an active, vocal block of voters can help mitigate interests that may attempt to undermine the desired outcome.

Political Will

Above all, political will is necessary to make something happen on Capitol Hill. But what is it? In this context, political will entails a commitment to the attainment of a political objective. How do we create the political will to focus on and adequately invest in long-term viable solutions to global problems such as the proliferation of weapons of mass destruction, human trafficking, and international civil conflict? If we care about these issues, we must translate our political will into a force for change among our elected leadership.

Political will, in its broadest sense, does not simply entail the decision-making priorities of professional politicians. The political life of a nation includes leaders in all segments of society— professional associations, small businesses, trade unions, religious institutions, and nongovernmental organizations, as well as individual citizens who choose to be involved. Creating political will among policymakers necessitates a coherent, knowledgeable political constituency comprised of any of the aforementioned actors willing to speak out.

In this context, it is important to understand the sometimes conflicting pressures between political will and political interest. For example, suppose a Member of Congress has a strong conservation ethic. She may have the political will to join an international parliamentarian group that focuses on global environmental concerns, yet receives criticism in the local press for every trip she takes abroad to meet with international colleagues and discuss these issues. This outcome is clearly not in her political interest. Conversely, her political interests may be served by wooing a large industry to the district that will create many jobs, even though this particular industry will pollute the nearby environment. Her political will is thus compromised by the contravening political interest. It is important for constituents to understand that the shorthand for political will is "taking a stand" despite the knowledge that one's political interests may not be served. An ideal situation for constituents is to find an issue where political will and political interests intersect. In our example, this would be bringing jobs to the district by wooing an environmental technology company or a business with a strong conservation ethic. In the realm of peace and security, this means demonstrating to your Member that time devoted to long-term peace and security challenges is in her political interest among an engaged and vocal constituency.

Developing a political constituency that will champion cooperative security and a balanced foreign policy toolkit requires clear and unambiguous signals of support from local leaders, community groups, and concerned citizens. Most importantly, political will for cooperative security will only result when voting behavior suggests a desire for it among a political constituency. Even if your Member of Congress has been successful in garnering federal funding for the new bridge downtown, do her views or voting record on foreign policy issues reflect your notion of responsible US leadership in the world? The momentum created by an engaged, informed constituency that supports cooperative engagement culminates in positive feedback for politicians, and this feedback will inevitably propel policymakers forward. An engaged constituency tells those elected that there is political support for time and effort spent on long-term solutions to international problems, and that these voters will "hang in there" with Members on the issues they care about. If the effect of a decision will cost the Member votes, she must—and will—pay attention.

Values versus Priorities

Most elected political leaders share common values. Nonviolent solutions to societal ills are widely agreed upon as preferable to sustained conflict, even by the most hardened skeptics. Such policies often fall under the heading of "prevention" and can best be understood through an analogy to an individual's health. We need to value investments in conflict prevention in the same way that we value our personal health. Exercise and good nutrition are key ingredients to longevity. But where security issues are concerned, we usually don't notice the problems until the patient is in the emergency room! Despite the values of a majority of Americans, the US often does not appear to be as invested in nonmilitary solutions and sustained approaches to addressing the roots of conflict—especially on the question of terrorism—as it is in assuring absolute military dominance over potential adversaries.[2] So why are the values of a majority often not reflected in the outcome on Capitol Hill?

This is an issue pitting values against priorities. One must clearly distinguish between the two, especially within the political context of Capitol Hill. While policymakers and their constituencies may hold the same fundamental values, translating those values into political action requires translating a specific

---

[2] Consider, for instance, that while Americans consider pure military capacity—always well-funded—an important component of the war on terror, they also heartily support a wide variety of nonmilitary approaches, many of which are invariably less well-funded. According to one recent poll: "An overwhelming 88% of Americans favor 'working through the UN to strengthen international laws against terrorism and to make sure UN members enforce them.' About the same number favor diplomatic efforts to apprehend suspects and dismantle terrorist training camps (89%) and setting up an international system to cut off funding for terrorism (89%). Nearly as many favor the trial of suspected terrorists in an International Criminal Court (83%) and diplomatic efforts to improve US relations with potential adversary countries (80%). In the same context, smaller but still substantial majorities favor making a major effort to be even-handed in the Israeli-Palestinian conflict (66%) and sharing intelligence information with other countries (58%). Even foreign aid is seen as an important means of combating terrorism. 'Helping poor countries develop their economies' is endorsed by 78% in order to combat terrorism." See "A World Transformed: Foreign Policy Attitudes of the US Public After September 11," Chicago Council on Foreign Relations and the German Marshall Fund of the United States, p. 8; available online at www.worldviews.org/docs/U.S.9-11v2.pdf.

value into a specific action or expectation, and then catapulting it to a priority on the agenda. There is no such thing, as the word "should" on Capitol Hill. Many people who work on foreign policy and security issues express astonishment that Congress does not exercise thorough oversight or take action on issues of concern to them. No matter how important any particular issue seems to the concerned citizen, there is no guarantee that Congress has the common good in mind in setting its priorities, or that the issue will actually get the consideration the general public thinks it deserves. While a two-way street exists between elected officials and the people they serve, "the US role in the twenty-first century must match the resources of the nation and the will of its people. An intensified dialogue between national leaders and the American people on issues like resources for foreign affairs and the use of force should seek to close the gap between views of the electorate and the way they are perceived by leaders in Washington."[3]

In closing the gap between the public and their elected leaders, the challenge will be to find politically meaningful ways to support general principles of US cooperative engagement in the world among a range of citizens who may hold differing views regarding specific solutions in any given case. Correspondingly, anyone organizing on behalf of international cooperation needs to take into account the different priorities competing for attention on Capitol Hill and adjust his strategy accordingly. A well-intentioned citizen can immediately undermine his objectives by not being cognizant of the time, budgetary, and structural constraints within which Members and their staffs operate.

Common Good versus Commercial Interest

A distinction must also be made between public interest in an outcome of common good and commercial interest in an outcome that benefits a specific group. Most citizens assume that their elected leaders are taking care of public interests like clean air, clean water, and a common defense. Most people would also agree that taking care of the common good means that leaders are not making decisions today that will compromise future

---

[3] Stanley Sloan, Mary Locke, and Casimir A. Yost, *The Foreign Policy Struggle: Congress and the President in the 1990s and Beyond* (Washington, DC: Institute for the Study of Diplomacy, Georgetown University, 2000), p. 10.

generations of Americans. Individuals who take it upon themselves to inspect the policy process a bit deeper are often astonished by how often those interests that get the best representation on Capitol Hill run counter to the common good. The motivating factors driving the decision-making process can be a cause for dismay, especially when it looks like the common good took a back seat to well-represented commercial interests.

Why do commercial interests often trump what seems to be an obvious public interest? The former have a profit motive that drives their interest in political representation, representation for which they pay large sums of money, both to political action committees and to savvy K Street lobbyists. Public interests rarely have the same financial wherewithal to elicit political representation. Instead, they rely on organized memberships and the sheer volume of less expensive grassroots tactics (petitions, letter-writing campaigns, etc.) to get their message across. Whereas both public and commercial interests might be lumped together in political rhetoric as "special interests," an uneven playing field exists when it comes to access and the capacity to influence priorities within Congress.

> "The fact that special interests can, and do, influence US foreign policy decisions is not perverse—it is one way that the US Government represents the interests of its citizens. In some cases, however, the influence of interest groups appears to go beyond what is reasonable, both from a democratic perspective and in terms of what makes good foreign policy. Perhaps the most troubling cases are those in which single-issue proponents have successfully diverted the debate and outcome to serve more narrow objectives."[4]

One special interest relevant to this discussion, the defense industry, has the specific advantage of being able to frame security through the lens of hardware and technology, items that lend themselves to linear and numerical notions of investments in security, and thereby concrete measures of "success." A defense lobbyist's pitch for an investment in "security" revolves around hardware and weapons platforms, tangible, readily measurable uses of taxpayer moneys. Those promoting the policy tools of soft

---

[4] Ibid., p. 29.

power to address current threats rarely share this advantage. For example, the "product" or measure of success related to establishing free and open media in fragile democracies is unlikely to be simple or straightforward. The "product" of these efforts may be of importance to the countries where new media outlets take root, but success does not confer measurable results for the district or state whose Member supports these activities.

The tendency for Congress to pay attention to defense-industry investments in security is also a result of a time-constrained environment where jobs in a district or state often take precedence over an innovative project in conflict prevention. In the daily agenda on Capitol Hill, taking time to talk to someone providing over 200 jobs in the district is much easier for a Member to justify than time spent with a public health expert wanting to discuss cost-effective approaches to training health officials in poor countries. The former is clearly in the Member's political interest and ranks high on the agenda; the latter, while potentially in line with the Member's political will, may also seem a waste of time with respect to her constituents' expectations.

A common technique used by the defense industry is to ensure that it has an organized presence in the districts of powerful Members, especially Members on the Armed Services Committees (or on the Subcommittees on Defense under the Appropriations Committees). For big weapons systems, the prime contractor will have subcontractors (i.e., jobs and money) situated in enough areas of the country to ensure that its aircraft, tank, missile system, or other asset is defended throughout the process of allocating defense dollars. If the technology involved is cutting-edge, an additional argument for supporting the program might involve potential applications of the technology in the civilian sector and added commercial opportunities in the district. In light of the obvious intersection between commercial and political interests, finding a champion (or several staunch and powerful proponents) for the Air Force's new tactical aircraft is much more straightforward than garnering sufficient support for efforts promoting primary education in the developing world, or providing commercial opportunities for nuclear or biological weapons scientists in Russia.

The terrorist attacks of September 11th made abundantly clear that we must consider social and political aspects of security with the same urgency that we do traditional military threats. After all, the root causes of terrorism exist in the social and political realm. We will not defeat this threat by military dominance alone, yet this realization has not shifted the immediate political interests and agenda-setting in Congress. Better fighter jets and more accurate missile technologies continue to be a much easier sell on Capitol Hill than additional funding for secular education in desperately poor areas of Pakistan, where free education is offered by radically anti-American religious leaders. Why the disconnect? We assert that the disconnect is largely a result of Cold War institutions, structural imbalances, and perceptions that impede a more effective approach to today's peace and security needs.[5]

A CHANGING WORLD AND CALCIFIED INSTITUTIONS

In order to better understand how these driving forces play out on Capitol Hill, it is important to discuss the Cold War framework for security, what remains unchanged within Congress, and the institutional factors that impede adaptation.

Hard Security Advantage

Over the past fifteen years, foreign-policy watchers witnessed the fall of the Berlin Wall, revolutions in Central Europe, and the dissolution of a nuclear-armed empire. During the 1990s, "nation-building" became an American security concern from Haiti to the former Yugoslavia. Once again genocide became part of the lexicon, if often veiled by the terminology of "ethnic cleansing." "Globalization" became associated with the changes we perceived happening around us, both for good and for ill. A new policy jargon developed as globalization accelerated: "failed states," "transnational threats," "non-state actors," "transitional governance," "virtual diplomacy," and the like. Academic experts and policy implementers took great interest in the tectonic shifts underway. But ironically, with the dissolution of the Soviet Union and the waning threat of nuclear war, interest in foreign policy atrophied significantly within Congress and among the general public.[6]

---

[5] Ibid., pp.30-31.
[6] Ibid., p. 1.

September 11th dramatically vaulted the American public and policymakers out of their comparatively low-key interest in foreign policy and illustrated the need for a vastly more complex and layered understanding of threats, as well as the need for new and different tools to adequately address them. In the post-September 11th security environment, threats are broadly distributed and "asymmetric": unpredictable; posed not just by nations but also by organizations and individuals; and targeted specifically at weaknesses and vulnerabilities. Security concerns run the gamut, from threats of cyberattacks on critical computer infrastructures to nuclear weapons in the hands of terrorist networks. US Government priorities, both domestic and international, must necessarily cover a broad spectrum as well. And the range of tools needed to adequately combat today's security threats runs from soft to hard.

The fact that security requires a balanced toolkit is not lost on today's servicemen and women. Indeed, many readers may find it surprising that the US military is remarkably progressive among our national security agencies. The US military represents a vast store of talented human resources; these resources have been consistently called upon to help solve many post-Cold War problems and fill a vacuum in the instruments available to achieve US foreign policy objectives.[7] But the complexity is also reflective of traditional military doctrine, which stresses a balance between civilian and military tools in problem solving. It is, after all, in the military's interest to be the policy tool of last resort.

The post-September 11th emphasis on military solutions to increasingly complex and diffuse security concerns has only aggravated longstanding Cold War (i.e., hard security) imbalances. While the priorities put forth in the President's defense budget often will be maintained throughout the legislative process, Congress, the holder of the "purse strings," currently lacks a unifying framework within which to assess priorities and

---

[7] "Long before September 11th, the US Government had grown increasingly dependent on its military to carry out its foreign affairs. The shift was incremental, little noticed, de facto. It did not even qualify as an 'approach.' The military simply filled a vacuum left by an indecisive White House, an atrophied State Department, and a distracted Congress." See Dana Priest, *The Mission: Waging War and Keeping the Peace with America's Military* (New York: W.W. Norton & Company, 2003), p. 14.

appropriately balance the investments in our "instruments of power."[8]

"National security" as a concept needs to be redefined for our post-Cold War and post-September 11th world. Issues like infectious disease, international crime, and terrorist networks do not fit into easy compartments or traditional rhetoric; their solutions require the effective application of all instruments of American power. Moreover, these challenges clearly belong on the menu of national security considerations. Although extensive work has been done since the end of the Cold War to document and better understand nontraditional threats, the findings of academic institutions and experts "in the field" have not yet translated into either widespread changes in public perceptions of both the problems and their appropriate solutions, or the political will necessary to achieve a well-stocked toolkit. The effective application of all our nation's instruments of power to address today's security challenges is the objective. Achieving this objective will require an ongoing dialogue between a dedicated, well-informed domestic constituency—one that must, above all, include military and civilian experts—and their elected leaders in Congress.

Cold War Rhetorical Framework

In order to fully appreciate the dramatic departure from tradition that today's security debate represents, as well as the structural changes required to address these new challenges, it is important to understand the policymaking context of the Cold War. For the many decades of the Cold War, the United States' security apparatus focused primarily on hard security needs. It was characterized by a state of antagonism and military conflict readiness between the US and the Soviet Union (USSR). The most famous artifact of the Cold War was the nuclear arms race between the two rivals. Cold War political rhetoric reinforced notions of hard security; nuclear weapons and their associated requirements mattered most in discussions of threats and responses. Congress was remarkably unified on both ensuring a nuclear advantage over

---

[8] According to the military's literature, the four core "instruments of power" are diplomacy, information, military and economics (or DIME). In other words, DIME are the instruments listed in the military's toolkit.

the Soviet Union as a hedge against weaker US conventional firepower, and on the importance of containing the communist threat.

"Containment" framed all aspects of official US security policy until the end of the Cold War. At the same time, many Americans participated in broad-based movements that offered alternatives to the framework. For example, whether one disagreed or agreed with the US intervention in Vietnam, it is clear today that widespread public discontent with US policies impacted elected leaders' decisions. Containment presented a clear case of either/or framing (i.e., "You're either with us or with the communists") and many citizens felt that elected leaders used the monolithic communist threat to obscure or distort other important issues. Many Americans mobilized against the militarization of US policy during this era and achieved significant victories, such as the inclusion of human rights concerns in mainstream issue debates. Further examples in which broad-based movements shifted policy are the push for an Anti-Ballistic Missile Treaty in the early 1970s and, in the 1980s, a negotiated peace for Central America and a well organized, effective nuclear freeze movement.

Understanding the Cold War framework for discussing security (as it applied in this earlier era) is important in order to avoid drifting into rhetoric inapplicable to today's dramatically different circumstances. One common categorization, for example, includes the labeling of policymakers as either "hawks" or "doves." This falsely poses security as a competition between hard and soft policy tools, and is an unhelpful distinction in the post-Cold War, post-September 11th world. Such terminology often arises in politically charged debates about who is "strong" on defense. The problem with using such language is that it restricts open, honest, and thorough debate. In order to shield themselves from accusations of being weak on defense or "not supporting the troops," nearly all elected leaders, whether Republican or Democrat, ask few critical questions in the process of approving hefty defense budgets. This happens even though the concerns of the so-called doves may be entirely valid. The hard power advantage was true during the Cold War, and it is still true now. Even though many soft issues are today more readily accepted as legitimate than during the Cold War years, they continue to be marginalized.

Today's unfortunate use of divisive language to frame peace and security issues is a legacy of the Vietnam War. The social implications are also severe, as many Americans continue to describe themselves as "anti- military." As anyone who has watched a presidential campaign can describe, during "hawks versus doves" debates, each side tends to shut out if not actively demonize the other. Each side also tends to frame hard and soft policy tools as competing, rather than complimentary or mutually reinforcing measures. It is our hope that this unproductive exchange of accusations does not transform itself to post-September 11th realities by pitting "well-stocked toolkit" advocates against "hard toolkit" traditionalists. Just as hawks and doves need to reassess and take a fresh look at the situation, those promoting balanced toolkit policy ideas need to develop effective strategies for breaking down barriers. At a local level, this might mean peace activists communicating with, or even collaborating with, veterans and individuals with recent military experience.[9]

The simplistic "us versus them" framework surfaced in the political discourse over priorities during the Cold War as well. For example, typical rhetoric for debating spending priorities during the Cold War was "guns versus butter." This dichotomous, zero-sum trade-off framed the reality of budget constraints as a competition between military and non- military expenditures. These trade-offs were usually depicted by a pie chart and budget figures, and the rhetoric was often overblown to score political points. Today, this zero-sum understanding with its focus on military solutions is inadequate. To address current challenges we need both "guns" and "butter" (i.e., hard and soft instruments) in our peace and security toolbox. And we need an honest and thorough debate regarding preventive foreign policies and programs as well as needed homeland security investments.

It is critical for readers to understand today's competing demands—international versus domestic, hard versus soft tools,

---

[9] It is important to understand the nature of military professionalism before asking uniformed or retired military to work with you. Part of the military ethic stresses non-obvious involvement in politics and avoiding any appearance of bias, which is why some professional military do not vote. That said, anyone with ground-truth experience in post-Cold War military missions is a treasure trove of information and knowledge. The key is tapping into this knowledge without threatening his sense of professionalism.

efforts at prevention abroad versus greater preparedness for the next terrorist attack at home, and so on. Of course, these competing demands inevitably will be framed as trade-offs. Should we, for instance, buy radiation detectors for use at US ports, or should we fund additional efforts to secure nuclear materials at the source?

In many instances, however, various policy options should not be perceived as trade-offs, but rather as different means to address the same concern. If we can eliminate the threat of "loose nukes" (weapons and fissile materials) by providing safeguards at vulnerable sites, then we have reduced the need to monitor cargo arriving at our ports. If failure is not an option, which approach has the greatest likelihood of success, and at what cost? Do we need both and, if so, at what levels of investment?

It is important to avoid language inapplicable to today's circumstances and to get beyond the Cold War standard of what it means to be "strong" on defense. It is equally important to rescue this discussion from the trade-off debate; what appear to be competing priorities may in fact be different approaches to mitigating the same threat. Further, we simply cannot continue to assume that the Cold War legacy bequeathed us the appropriate mix and resource allocations for our policy instruments.

This last point underscores the importance of a carefully considered and positive strategy for educating Congress on peace and security. Unless a broader set of policy tools to address a range of challenges is seen as a vital part of our post-September 11th security strategy, present day imbalances will remain, and strategies that we care deeply about—like a balanced role for the military and sufficient investments in preventive efforts—will become victims of political rhetoric. We need an informed dialogue about competing security challenges, and the most effective means to address them. With a systematic and rational adjustment of our priorities, there is no reason Americans cannot expect a federal government to meet their needs at home and abroad.[10]

---

[10] In recent years, numerous coalitions have formed to address the need for US global engagement. These coalitions cut across traditional issue advocacy boundaries (e.g., the environment, nuclear nonproliferation, or anti-poverty) to stress the overarching theme of teamwork and cooperation as a US security

Institutional Factors

As a result of our dozen years of combined experience on Capitol Hill, we are convinced that the imbalance in our policymaking process is not a partisan issue. Rather, it is a product of an inflexible institution with limited time and even less ability to understand issues in a complicated context. This imbalance is also the inevitable product of an institution that will almost always choose the path of least resistance (i.e., favor the status quo). While built-in traditional and procedural rigidities are a cause, turf and power issues also come into play. [11]

Congress is a competitive environment, in which the beneficiaries of hard-security solutions are very well organized and well funded. For every local political science professor or veteran visiting Capitol Hill, a staffer probably will hear from numerous defense lobbyists, especially if his Member serves on one of the defense committees. The defense industry lobbies provide a good example of expert representation, one that should be emulated to the extent possible. For example, the defense industry has a built-in constituency in most districts; it keeps its military hardware items visible through advertising and lobbying; its sales pitch is always tailored to current events; and it builds coalitions among its own segments as well as between congressional offices, if necessary. While many of its creations are necessary and important components of meeting emerging security challenges, its sophisticated tactics and influence flowing from jobs and dollars in the district have the unfortunate side effect of directing disproportionate attention to hardware-focused solutions.

An illustration of this tendency is seen when technological solutions to security problems (e.g., unmanned aerial vehicles) are prioritized over low-tech solutions (e.g., foreign-language training for US intelligence and foreign service officers). The irony of this particular example is that with the increase in technological collection capability within our intelligence agencies, a corresponding annual 30% growth in the need for foreign language

---

interest; such new partnership is vital. See, for instance, www.usintheworld.org (available summer 2004) and www.usgloballeadership.org.
[11] Colton C. Campbell and Nicole C. Rae, eds., *New Majority or Old Minority?: The Impact of Republicans on Congress* (Lanham, Maryland: Rowman and Littlefield, 1999), pp. 76-90.

capacity is expected.[12]   If we have the best collection capability and the fastest fighter jets, their application is for naught without the longer-term health of the institutions and necessary investments in training.   Such realities are a clear example of focusing on the high-tech hardware end of the spectrum to the detriment of the human capital investments necessary to succeed.

Despite the commercial interests that often parallel our elected leaders' political interests, all agree that it is the people in our military who are our most important asset. If we spend too much on military hardware at the expense of training, educating, and retaining the people in our armed forces, the institution will eventually fail. Moreover, we would deprive the policy process of experienced and knowledgeable resources. The educational and training needs of military professionals, plus their role as partners in achieving better balance will be a vital part of effectively addressing today's security challenges.

An additional institutional problem is that Congress is often reactive. The challenge for those who want to educate on peace and security is therefore this: When prevention succeeds, nothing happens. Or, stated differently, peace is a non-event. So how do we give concrete meaning to long-term security efforts that are not just a reaction to the latest headline, and instead offer to Members proof of a tangible return on the taxpayer's investment?   If a program's effectiveness is evidenced by what does not happen, how does one provide proof of success?

Sometimes groups interested in peace and security assume that because theirs is a general issue of public concern, Members of Congress will devote adequate attention to it. This is not so. As a Member of Congress once said to a large audience of nuclear nonproliferation activists, "This place is a stimulus-response institution—if you push the right buttons, you can get what you want out of it."   With these words, the Member exhorted the listeners to organize, to support public institutions that work on reducing the dangers of nuclear weapons, and to bring these issues consistently into the mainstream by avoiding technical or inaccessible language. He was also telling the audience to develop

---

[12] Government Accounting Office, *Foreign Languages: Human Capital Approach Needed to Correct Staffing and Proficiency Shortfalls* (Washington, DC: Government Accounting Office, January 2002), p. 12.

an outreach strategy and to become a visible constituency in order to credibly hold their own Members of Congress accountable.

The peace and security community needs to understand what buttons to push. It also needs a sophisticated and organized outreach campaign that represents diverse viewpoints regarding the broad spectrum of tools needed to address today's security challenges. Is it possible to emulate the expert representation and tactical behavior of the defense industry in educating elected leaders? While it will probably have less financial means at its disposal, money is not essential to create political will. We assume there is, in fact, a built-in and as yet untapped constituency for these concerns—from local Guard units to veterans' organizations to conflict resolution practitioners to church missionary groups. What is missing, in many cases, is sufficient organization within the peace and security community to make sure the word gets out in a coherent and compelling way.

Institutional Changes and the Decline of Policy Capacity

At heart, Congress is not an institution with an international outlook. After all, Congress, and especially the House of Representatives, was not set up to focus on issues beyond US borders. The 435 representatives are sent to Washington by voters to service local interests. The Senate has a more international outlook, and senators often aspire to statesman-like tasks. In addition, this "upper body" of Congress has obligatory international duties such as ratifying treaties. However, despite numerous polls demonstrating widespread public support for active US engagement in the world, issues such as preventive action and international cooperation remain abstract and of low priority to many Members of Congress. Unless constituents make these issues understandable and important, neither representatives nor senators will perceive a stake in having a strong opinion one way or the other. Hence, there is little reason for a Member to do anything beyond agreeing that these issues are indeed important and then proceeding to vote the party line.[13]

Long-term institutional trends, in conjunction with changes made in the mid-1990s, have short-circuited careful deliberation of

---

[13] Sloan, Locke and Yost, *The Foreign Policy Struggle: Congress and the President in the 1990s and Beyond*, p. 23.

important policy issues and diminished Congress' ability to perform oversight. Many of the institutional trends have been underway for several decades and others reflect shifts in society or in the electorate, but "both parties bear considerable responsibility" for the decline in the institution's policymaking capacity.[14] Such institutional trends include the general erosion of the committee process and the drift in power and influence from *authorization* committees (those that set policy) to *appropriations* committees (those that allocate the annual budget). In both the House and Senate, party leaders increasingly bypass the committee of jurisdiction by bringing important authorization bills directly to the floor. In other instances, policy matters that should be handled by an authorization committee are attached to one of the thirteen must-pass appropriations bills as a "rider."[15] Whereas committees used to be "the preeminent centers of legislative ideas and decision-making," majority-party leaders have written more and more bills in recent decades or a small number of Members closely aligned with the leadership.[16]

As we have noted, absent the threat of nuclear annihilation, international policy issues became less urgent with the end of the Cold War. The International Relations Committee in the House (HIRC) and the Foreign Relations Committee in the Senate (SFRC) became less desirable choices for Members. Members increasingly seek committees that will allow them to bring home the money to their district or state, resulting in high turnover and diminished experience on the committees responsible for foreign policy. This is significant because the HIRC and the SFRC are authorizing committees, which means that they provide the forum for deliberating and reflecting on complex policy issues and setting big-picture policy. As such, they provide a vital venue for framing issues and priorities, and for understanding international issues. This is true for the committees that oversee foreign relations and defense, as well as all other policy areas. Lastly, the shift in power from policy committees to money committees not only degrades

---

[14] Richard E. Cohen, Kirk Victor, and David Baumann, "The State of Congress," *National Journal*, vol. 36, no. 2 (January 10, 2004): p. 86.

[15] A rider is an amendment unrelated to the subject matter of the measure to which it is attached. This often happens with policy items attached to appropriations bills.

[16] Cohen, Victor, and Baumann, "The State of Congress," p. 89.

the deliberative process of legislation, but it also leaves the policymaking process more vulnerable to special interests and overall imbalance.[17]

The vulnerability created by this shift is partly a result of highly restricted channels of information and communication. For example, the institutional feedback process through which Members of Congress exercise their prerogative of oversight is the committee hearing. The hearing process provides an important venue for official, on-the-record testimony from government agencies and others to report to Congress. Hearings also provide a venue for diverse viewpoints to be laid out, albeit one ultimately controlled by the majority party. Yet the formal, protocol-laden process of committee hearings frequently fails to provide a good problem-solving venue. Indeed, communication is constrained by rigid formalities, such as majority/minority hierarchy, White House talking points, and Members' constant awareness of the media's presence. In many ways, committee procedures impede mutually beneficial settlements of problems or challenges. In fact, hearings can sometimes add to the adversarial environment of Capitol Hill just as much as they alleviate it through new knowledge and understanding.

The diminished role of the authorization committees and consolidation of power within the leadership in the mid-1990s have led to the frequent assertion that the committee process is in fact broken. "As the century ends," one analysis argues,

> "the breakdown of the committee system has become a major factor in the chaos that pervades Capitol Hill. Congressional leaders repeatedly have encountered difficulties with party-driven legislation that was hastily brought to the House or Senate floor without a thorough vetting—or any attempts at bipartisan compromise— among experts at the committee level."

He continues:

---

[17] For more discussion of this shift, see Richard E. Cohen, Kirk Victor and David Baumann, "The State of Congress," *National Journal*, vol. 36, no. 2 (January 10, 2004).

"In recent years, a growing number of Members seeking to learn about issues have often found committee hearings so stage-managed as to be useless, and these Members have stopped relying on the committees as a source for education and deliberation. In one alternative approach, small groups of Members get together and call experts to their offices for private discussions."[18]

Beyond the loss of this relatively simple Cold War framework and consensus, a Republican-controlled Congress clashed with a Democratic White House between 1995 and 2001. During this period in particular, many issues fell victim to mistrust between Congress and the executive branch and to partisan posturing. Instead of comprising a well-considered debate about post-Cold War priorities and a common plan to move forward, foreign policy too often became a casualty of partisan politics. (Such politicking happens on both the left and the right. For example, in 1991, Democrat Bill Clinton attacked incumbent President George Bush for spending too much time on foreign policy. A few years later, Republicans on the Hill used the *Contract With America* to lambaste President Clinton for US involvement in peacekeeping and other non-traditional military missions.)

Foreign policy and security concerns were also casualties of institutional changes in the last decade. In 1995, the new GOP leadership adopted rules for the 104th Congress that reformed many aspects of staffing, committee jurisdiction, and internal legislative service organizations in the House of Representatives. An unfortunate side effect of these changes was to significantly cut back on congressionally supported ways for Members to become informed or act on cooperative international issues.[19] Before 1995, a system of bipartisan issue-caucuses and legislative service organizations within Congress supported Members and their staffs on special topics like hunger, military reform, foreign policy, and arms control. These caucuses operated outside the official committees and were staffed by individuals funded and shared by

---

[18] Richard E. Cohen, "Crackup of the Committees," *National Journal*, vol. 30, no. 31 (July 31, 1999).
[19] Campbell and Rae, eds., *New Majority or Old Minority?: The Impact of Republicans on Congress*, p. 76.

all caucus members, both Republican and Democrat. These venues offered opportunities for Members to be involved in issues and meet other colleagues with similar interests outside of the committee of jurisdiction. They amplified opportunities for collegial cooperation and improved bipartisanship as well.

In 1995, the caucus system was changed so that funding for all specialized staff positions was eliminated. Caucuses were still allowed to exist, but without funding for dedicated Hill staff. This dramatically reduced the caucuses' ability to actually do anything other than be listed as contacts in the Senate and House telephone directories. Some caucuses became private nongovernmental entities (located off Capitol Hill) with differing levels of success. Without dedicated, full-time staff to reserve rooms, organize meetings, vet speakers, and communicate to interested parties in both the House and Senate, the caucus system was rendered bereft of the substantive staff necessary to coordinate bipartisan collaboration on important issues. In almost every instance the ability of the caucuses to be active on substantive issues inside Congress was severely cut back.

As one powerful exception to the rule, today's Congressional Hunger Center exemplifies how dedicated Members and nongovernmental activists sustained their issue despite institutional setbacks. The Center originated as a Select Committee on Hunger, founded in 1984 by a bipartisan group of House Members determined to do something about domestic and international hunger and poverty. In 1993 a number of the select committees, including the one on hunger, were abolished, so the group reconstituted itself as the Hunger Caucus in Congress and simultaneously started an off-the-Hill organization called the Congressional Hunger Center.[20] When the caucus system's substantive, full-time staff was eliminated in 1995, the Center took up many of the education and outreach tasks to keep its issue alive on Capitol Hill.

A list of Congressional Membership Organizations can be found online.[21] This listing illustrates the myriad interests of Members and provides an overview of issue areas that probably depend on outside organizations to support their profile on the Hill.

---

[20] For more information, see www.hungercenter.org.
[21] For more information, see www.house.gov/cha/publications/ publications.html.

It is also important to know that the number of caucuses and Congressional Membership Organizations is not fixed—and Members (or staffers) can initiate new ones.

The previously mentioned reforms also eliminated the Office of Technology Assessment (OTA), which during its twenty-three years in operation provided nonpartisan analysis of complex scientific and technical issues—from fusion energy to technology in teaching to electronic surveillance. OTA served as the key resource for Members and staffers confronting scientific or technological issues relevant to public policy.[22] As scientific expertise is not readily available to all Members, to say nothing of nonpartisan analysis on scientific matters, the loss of OTA greatly diminished Congress' capacity to address the implications of technological advances on public policy.

The disappearance of the caucus system and the elimination of OTA, combined with the downsizing of committee and Congressional Research Service staff, left far fewer individuals with substantive and specialist backgrounds actually working for Congress. Meanwhile, leadership staffs were augmented, allowing more partisan influence on substantive issues. These reforms both lowered the priority of having foreign policy expertise on personal staffs and diminished the profile of cooperative security issues overall.

Despite all of the innovative cooperative programs happening within our own government during the 1990s (e.g., nuclear weapons dismantlement in the former Soviet Union, rule-of-law assistance to young democracies, military assistance through NATO's Partnership for Peace program), information about many such programs often did not filter up to the Congress. Lacking intermediaries, an organized lobby, and a coherent message, and confronting powerful ideological opponents, cooperative international strategies have languished.

These cumulative actions—together with an often acrimonious and partisan climate—have contributed to the decline of international policy capacity in Congress. Overcoming structural imbalances and entrenched perceptions within the time-constrained, rigid institutions on the Hill presents a formidable

---

[22] For more information, see www.access.gpo.gov/ota/ or www.wws.princeton. edu/~ota/.

challenge. September 11th sent all Members and staffers scrambling to catch up on many foreign policy and security issues, a process that continues today. Remember, the common denominator today is uncertainty. Congress is undergoing a learning process, and change will take time. But an engaged and well-informed constituency, focused both on broadly shared security concerns and on balance within our policy toolkit, can help guide and expedite the learning process.

The chapters that follow will offer resources, tips, and tools for those interested in being the well-informed constituents who make cooperative international issues coherent and compelling, inspiring elected officials to become more active on the issues that you care about.

— 3 —

From the Inside Looking Out

Now that we have briefly covered Congress in today's context, we turn to the issues of majority party, leadership, power, and the many hats a Member of Congress wears. In the various roles a Member plays, his performance will be subject to the chamber in which he serves (i.e., House or Senate), whether the Member's party is currently in the majority or minority, expectations of the party leadership, and other factors. A general understanding of the main factors that enhance or constrain a Member's actions is fundamental to one's understanding of Capitol Hill and an accurate assessment of entry points and opportunities to shape the debate.

In this assessment, we will generalize broadly about what are often unique circumstances related to a particular Member's power, personality, and interests, the level of expertise of the Member and his staff, and the interests of the constituencies that the Member serves. It is therefore critical to familiarize yourself with your representative or senator before approaching his office. Understanding the context in which he operates, the roles he is expected to play, and the daily demands on Members and their staffs is an essential element in formulating one's strategy.

This chapter will use two fictional case studies in order to help you think through how party affiliation, power, and roles performed by a Member and the media apply to peace and security efforts. Our intent in the use of these case studies is to assist you in viewing the institution from the inside looking out and to coach you in thinking like a Member (or his staffer) in order to devise creative options on how to help the Member help you.

CASE STUDY ONE: PEACE AND CONFLICT STUDIES

You are a well-established professor of conflict resolution. Last year you were given a wonderful but challenging task: Establish a peace and conflict studies program at your university, a state institution that serves a diverse population in the Rocky Mountain West. You have been involved in peace studies for many years, but you have also been active as a practicing mediator in the community. It is important to you that both the theory and the practice of peacemaking are understood as inseparable and important. Your organization has many resources to offer to an interested policymaker. After just one year in existence, you have students eager to become more involved in international issues, as well as a student-organized conflict resolution service on campus. Within your immediate reach are not only theoretical and practical knowledge, but also several bright, eager students who would like to be involved in applying what they are learning in your program to international issues of peace and conflict.

In your view Congress does not appear to recognize the possible role of conflict resolution in addressing current global security challenges. You have repeatedly witnessed how indicators of an impending conflict were ignored until the situation exploded into a full-blown crisis requiring an international response. How would you approach a Member of Congress about your program and the role of conflict resolution in mitigating crises, preventing atrocities, and lowering the long-term costs of intervention? Is your representative in the majority party in the House? If not, what about your senator? How might you tie your program's efforts to issues of broad public concern? What opportunities might you offer to your Member that would be mutually beneficial to him and to your program?

CASE STUDY TWO: BIKES AND BANDAGES ABROAD

You are a bike shop owner in New England. Five years ago, you visited an impoverished Caribbean country as part of a humanitarian mission organized by your church. When you returned, you decided to do something practical based on the advice of a local teenager you met while on the mission. This young local, Sami, wistfully told you, "I could go to school in the next village if only I could get there." Later that year, you brought up this issue while sitting at a high school basketball game with the school's nurse. By the following year, you and the school nurse developed a partnership to collect used bikes and excess medical supplies and to deliver them once a year to Sami's village and nearby communities.

This program was an instant low-cost, high-impact hit. Numerous individuals in the local community, including many in your church community, jumped on board to advertise the need, donate bikes and medical supplies, and raise funds for transport of the donated items to their destination. High school kids raised money to help pay the freight costs, learning valuable lessons about poverty in the developing world and the role of nongovernmental actors as part of US efforts abroad. Several students recently asked if they could accompany you to deliver the goods, and the school nurse has several colleagues who would like to accompany you and offer their medical expertise for hands-on training in these communities. In addition, three months ago your best friend, who is a Civil Affairs Officer with the National Guard, returned from a yearlong deployment to Afghanistan. She became very excited upon hearing about the success of your project and wants to duplicate it for a small town in Afghanistan.

Although duplication of this project for a village in Afghanistan might be entirely feasible without getting politicians involved, might your congresswoman be interested in the project's success in the Caribbean and helpful in efforts to expand to a country currently in the headlines? Is your congresswoman well positioned to be of assistance in these efforts? What aspects of the program could be highlighted to garner her support? What are the expectations and constraints she might confront in trying to support these efforts?

INSTITUTIONAL PARAMETERS

Majority and Leadership

In both the House and Senate, the majority party controls all committee chairs and controls the legislative agenda. Both the Democratic and Republican Party leaderships use carrots and sticks alike to maintain party discipline. The party leadership in both chambers is also responsible for fostering cooperation, building coalitions, and sometimes, facilitating compromise. At the same time, the House is much more dominated by the majority than the Senate. This difference results largely from the role of the Rules Committee and prerogatives of the majority in the House, as compared to the consensus-based legislative process in the Senate. Senators have statewide and national constituencies; representatives focus heavily on local issues and formulate agendas highly tailored to their constituencies. While the Senate tends to be more deliberative, the House is generally more partisan and ideological. This trend in the House leads to greater party cohesion and frequent party-line votes on issues.[1]

Presiding Officers

The Speaker of the House is the leader of the majority party as well as the chamber's presiding officer. These dual roles allow the Speaker to use his parliamentary and political powers to govern proceedings on the floor. He recognizes—or refuses to recognize—Members to speak. In the Senate, the presiding officer is formally the vice president, as provided in Article 1 of the Constitution. The Constitution further stipulates that a "President *pro tempore*" preside in the vice president's absence.[2] In reality, however, only rarely does either the vice president or the president *pro tempore* preside over Senate proceedings. The vice president typically presides only when he might be needed to break a tied vote on an issue of great importance to the White House. The president *pro tempore* exercises his right to appoint a senator as "Acting President *pro tempore*," and that senator can then appoint still another to serve as Acting President *pro tempore*. The duty of presiding officer in the Senate is routinely filled by a rotation of junior or first-term senators of the majority party for one-hour intervals.[3]

Because the presiding officer in the Senate is not necessarily an official member of the body, presiding in this instance does not confer the same powers in terms of recognition and controlling floor proceedings. The Senate's presiding officer may speak only if granted permission by "unanimous consent,"[4] and he must recognize the first senator standing and seeking recognition. In the

---

[1] A "party-line" vote refers to alignment on the issue being a result of party membership—all Republicans vote one way and all Democrats the other.

[2] The president *pro tempore* is the most senior senator of the majority party and is elected by a majority vote in the Senate. See Mary E. Mulvihill, *House and Senate Rules of Procedure: A Comparison* (Washington, DC, Congressional Research Service Report 97-270GOV, February 1997), p. 7.

[3] Mulvihill, *House and Senate Rules of Procedure: A Comparison*, pp. 6-7.

[4] "Unanimous consent" refers to a procedure for expedited consideration of a measure: All Members agree to the measure so long as no individual Member objects. See David Silverberg, *Congress for Dummies* (New York: Wiley Publishing, Inc., 2002), p. 331.

case that several senators simultaneously seek recognition, preferential recognition goes to the majority and minority leaders, and then the majority and minority floor managers.[5] Control of Senate floor proceedings is maintained only through building consensus between the majority and minority parties and through accommodating individual senators' wishes on an ongoing basis.

Majority Party and Procedure

Ample publications explain in detail the procedures, rules, and traditions that guide the legislative process and agenda-setting within Congress.[6] What is most important to understand is that in the House, the majority rules when party cohesion is maintained; conversely, collegiality and consensus are fundamental to the legislative process in the Senate. This is especially true when majority status rests on only a very slim margin, as has been the case in the past several years. The House maintains a very structured legislative process, with strict adherence to the chamber's rules and precedents needed to manage the decision-making process for 435 representatives. The Senate's smaller numbers allow for more flexibility in its approach to the standing rules. Whereas representatives typically must yield to the will of the majority, any senator's individual legislative priorities will often be accommodated in some fashion.

The different processes each chamber uses to structure floor consideration of bills reveal the House's premium on the power of the majority will and the Senate's premium on the power of individual senators. "Special rules" establish the conditions governing floor deliberations on most legislative measures in the House. The House Rules Committee determines the rules for debate, such as the amount of "floor time," whether amendments will be "in order" (allowed), limitations on debate, and possibly, a

---

[5] The "floor manager" in the Senate attempts to coordinate deliberations on specific legislation.

[6] See Michael L. Koempel and Judy Schneider, *Congressional Deskbook 2003-2004*, (Alexandria, VA, The Capitol.Net; 2003). For online resources, see: http://www.thecapitol.net/PublicPrograms/als.html. Also, the State Department makes several publications from the *Congressional Research Service* available on-line at: http://usinfo.state.gov/usa/infousa/laws/majorlaw/s98-94.htm

waiver of "points of order"[7] against specific provisions. In the Senate these parliamentary conditions are specified by a "unanimous consent" agreement that functions similarly to a "special rule" in House procedure. The major distinction is that unanimous consent agreements are negotiated by the majority leader in consultation with the minority leader, committee chairmen, and interested senators. All senators must accept a unanimous consent agreement; an objection by any senator can prevent the agreement from taking effect. This gives any interested senator the opportunity to thwart all legislative action—by refusal to agree to a unanimous consent or through use of a filibuster—until his concerns are adequately addressed.[8] Of course, any senator who considers throwing himself on the legislative train tracks for a cause must carefully balance the political costs with respect to all other legislative priorities on the list. Abusing the prerogative of individual power can quickly undermine his longer-term effectiveness within the institution.

Legislative Agenda

As mentioned earlier, the leadership sets the legislative agenda in both chambers. Agenda-setting is, however, not solely a matter of making a list and moving bills to the floor in sequence. This ever-changing agenda will be shaped by numerous factors, including the President's priorities, public expectations, and the pressure brought to bear by powerful Members. Two realities inevitably hold sway. First, each year the Congress is *supposed* to pass a budget resolution and *must* pass thirteen appropriations bills, either as stand-alone spending bills or as part of an "omnibus," to complete the budget. The annual budget process alone consumes an immense amount of Congress' floor time. Second, the agenda of the Senate majority is always subject to the possibility that

---

[7] A "point of order" is an "objection to a current proceeding, measure or amendment because the proposed action violates a rule of the chamber, written precedent, or rule-making statute." See Koempel and Schneider, *Congressional Deskbook 2003-2004: 108th Congress*, p. 578. For example, points of order are often raised against bills thought to violate the budget resolution by exceeding the funding amount set forth for federal spending in a given fiscal year.

[8] A filibuster is a time-delaying tactic associated with the Senate and used by the minority to delay, modify or defeat a bill or amendment. A filibuster can only occur in the absence of a unanimous consent. Mulvihill, *House and Senate Rules of Procedure: A Comparison*, p. 5.

amendments not directly pertaining to the purpose of a legislative item will be offered during its consideration, unless precluded by the governing unanimous consent agreement for that item. [9] Setting the agenda is always a process of backroom negotiations, coalition-building on must-pass items, and horse-trading to avoid unhappy surprises in the outcome, especially in the Senate.

In Chapter 2 we discussed the difference between values and priorities on Capitol Hill. The majority party's priorities can be identified by what items are placed at the top of the legislative agenda. Legislative priorities must be squeezed into an already tight calendar, made more so by must-pass bills, White House priorities and possible emergencies. These constraints make time for floor consideration of specific legislative items rare and, therefore, valuable.

Most priorities are obvious and directly reflect a must-pass budgetary item, a political imperative due to public pressure and expectations (such as emergency federal assistance to combat forest fires), or a political opportunity. For instance, the fact that a comprehensive restructuring of US foreign assistance has not been addressed since 1985 reflects the (lack of) priority placed on the role of non-military engagement in achieving US objectives abroad. This contrasts with the fact that, in most years, the defense appropriations legislation is the first spending bill passed by both chambers and signed into law by the president.

Party, Power, and Political Capital

A Member's political position is determined by party politics, seniority, and the committees on which he serves. It is important to consider each of these items to gauge the potential role he might perform in promoting a particular policy or cause. Floor debates and voting decisions are largely dictated by the party. Party loyalty confers the privileges—such as advancement to leadership

---

[9] A Member will be constantly seeking a good "vehicle" for his legislative priorities. A vehicle is a "legislative measure that is being considered," the term being used usually in a Senate context where amendments and riders can be attached. See Koempel and Schneider, *Congressional Deskbook 2002-2003*, p. 581. For example, during the first session of the 108th Congress, the State Department reauthorization bill failed to be considered on the floor due to a threat to amend this State Department bill (vehicle) with a minimum wage amendment.

or plum committee assignments—most Members find necessary to advance their own position of power within the institution. If a Member votes against the dictates of his party, there will be consequences at some point in the future such as a desired committee assignment not awarded, a bypassed legislative priority or an alienated group of colleagues. Very few Members can afford to be renegades on a continual basis.

Because seniority plays such an important role in both chambers, longstanding Members can mitigate some of the costs of being a rebel. The seniority system generally allows Members to accumulate power proportionate to their longevity in office. The more powerful a Member becomes, the more likely she is to attain committee chairmanships and leadership positions within the party. In addition, greater seniority confers increased contacts, a greater fundraising base, name recognition, and more frequent media coverage. In some cases, however, power and ability to break ranks is unrelated to seniority or committee membership, and is based instead on a Member's personal experience. Senator John McCain (a prisoner of war during Vietnam), former senator Bob Kerrey (a decorated Vietnam veteran), and former senator Max Cleland (a triple amputee from his own service in that war) all have more credibility and political latitude on questions of peace and security due to their personal histories. Senator (and currently Majority Leader) Bill Frist, a medical doctor, played a leadership role during the Senate anthrax crisis, and he has successfully championed the Bush Administration's HIV/AIDS initiative.

Accurately assessing real power in Congress is anything but a straightforward calculation. In addition, the power constellation shifts with each election when leadership and committee assignments change. Even though the importance of seniority permeates both chambers, it also differs between them. While the post-Watergate House reforms of 1974 devolved power from committee chairmen to individual representatives, "over the past decade the Speaker and his leadership team have once again become more powerful."[10] With the Republican takeover of the House in 1994, the seniority system was shaken up. Whereas earlier committee chairmen could serve unlimited terms, the new rules limit chairmanship to no more than three terms. In addition, chairmanships are now determined by a process of interviews with

---

[10] Hamilton, *How Congress Works and Why You Should Care*, p. 63.

the leadership rather than by seniority. These procedural changes increased the power of leadership and decreased the role of committees, especially authorizing committees. These changed rules and procedures in the House for moving legislative proposals have made the challenge of promoting alternative views all the greater. These changes also make bipartisan efforts more difficult because the majority leadership can bypass committee chairmen. [11]

How should you think about process, party politics, and power in formulating a strategy? First, it is important to remember that all Members, regardless of seniority, committee assignments, or gravitas on a subject, have finite political capital. [12] An investment of any increment of their political capital on a particular issue will be based on a complex calculation of constituent support, party politics and long-term costs and benefits. A senator with six years between election campaigns will have a very different calculation from a representative whose two-year term essentially means the campaigning never ceases. Anyone promoting a particular policy option—especially in the current environment—needs to be realistic about garnering majority support. It is highly unlikely that any legislative item will move forward without majority party support in the House. Again, the Senate is a different story.

Let's look at our two case studies to see how these institutional parameters apply to one's assessment.

CASE STUDY ONE: PEACE AND CONFLICT STUDIES

After some initial research, you discover that your Member of Congress does not appear very engaged on peace and security issues. He does not serve on any of the defense or foreign policy committees and is quoted in a newspaper article as being "proud that I've never had a passport." Although his party is in the majority, you are not very optimistic that he will care about the resources you could offer. However, before you give up, ask yourself these questions: Whom can you partner with to make this offer seem more appealing? A local veterans' group? Are there any Reserve Officers Training Corps or recently deployed students

---

[11] Rae and Campbell, eds., *New Majority or Old Minority?*, pp. 89-90.

[12] "Political capital" is the sum total of all tangible and intangible factors that enable leaders to get anything done, including reputation, media attention, statutory role, friends and networks, fundraising ability, and so forth.

in your classes? Alternatively, try using a more local angle. What has been the success rate of the mediation services on campus? Are these services saving the university money? How many conflict resolution programs exist in the Member's district? Does your local criminal justice system use mediators? How much does this save the district as a whole? A solid local hook to demonstrate the growing importance of conflict resolution—both its local applications and its international implications—can help the Member understand the tangible value of your program.

Think creatively about what you might offer to interest a Member. You could, for example, propose any one of the following "services" to the Member:

- Offer a cost-free intern from your university to help on conflict resolution/peacekeeping for the Member, and give the student credit toward graduation for Capitol Hill experience;[13]

- Be the Member's support organization on issues of conflict prevention or peacekeeping, available at a moment's notice to the Member and his staff;

- Keep abreast of bills being offered in the House and Senate that support international conflict resolution, and make your expert advice on these legislative items available to the Member on a timely basis;

- Offer the opportunity for the Member to pitch your school's program to other districts (this can make for an exciting leadership opportunity for the Member);

---

[13] Numerous positions and advisory roles on Capitol Hill are staffed by "fellows." Academic institutions in particular can leverage these positions to improve their internal understanding of Congress and to offer a great learning experience for students or faculty. In addition, since expertise is usually quite thin on the personal staffs in Congress (especially in the House) and since budgets for staff are limited, Members often welcome the possibility of retaining such experts free of charge. See ethics standards for the House and Senate for the rules that apply to this possibility at http://www.house.gov/ethics/ and http://ethics.senate.gov/.

- Agree to prepare continually updated memos on the Member's top three international issues;

- Conduct a yearly local poll on local citizens' interest in international cooperation issues; or

- Keep track of the peace-and-conflict-related jobs in the district, including activities of local Guard and Reserve units, local businesses with international activities, exchange programs, etc.

If you think the Member's views are far from your own, keep looking for ways to define the issue that are easier for the Member to entertain. For example, you can work with other local groups that care about the issues, approach other mediation programs in the local community, find tangible examples that demonstrate the value of your program, and then follow up with logical next steps if possible. If you do not have a group already organized to press your issue, you could use a petition, letter-writing campaign or visits to the Member of Congress as a way to get one started. Try not to approach this in a hostile manner. Members of Congress do not mind getting mail, petitions, and the like, so long as your approach is respectful and you give them a way to respond that allows them to appear in a positive light.[14] Always try the positive approach first. If your Member already shares your views, strategize together about the next steps and try to get him to help you expand the constituency for your views.

CASE STUDY TWO: BIKES AND BANDAGES ABROAD

According to your initial research about your congresswoman, not only is she in the minority party, but she also does not serve on any committees directly relevant to international affairs. However,

---

[14] Regular mail is the least efficient. Since the anthrax attacks in 2001, mail is first sent to the Midwest for irradiation before reaching Capitol Hill. Fax and email are far superior. In addition, the motto in many offices regarding incoming mail is this: "Only put as much effort into the response as went into the original letter." In other words, a form letter from one hundred constituents will get one hundred uniform responses in return and probably little action beyond that.

you did come across her name as the co-chair of the Women's Caucus in the House Directory and found a couple of press releases detailing speeches she had given on the importance of women's rights in economic development and security efforts abroad, especially in Islamic countries. In light of your current desire to expand this program to Afghanistan, the educational opportunities for girls in remote villages would appear to be an appropriate hook. In addition, access to health care for women, although still not a core mission of your organization, could be made a central theme for the program's mission in Afghanistan.

Again, however, as your congresswoman is in the minority, how can you get a buy-in from the majority? What positions do your senators hold? Does either of them belong to the majority party or serve on a relevant committee? How are relations between your congresswoman and the rest of the state's delegation in DC?[15] Is there any particular relationship between your congresswoman and a senator that could serve as a bipartisan and bicameral duo to advance your efforts? If not, could you help your congresswoman to use statements and priorities related to US efforts in Afghanistan as a hook for majority interest? The issue of weak states as security risks has been repeatedly highlighted by high-level policy officials in the executive branch and by the majority leadership in Congress. For example, the preface to the 2002 National Security Strategy stated: "The events of September 11, 2001 taught us that weak states, like Afghanistan, can pose as great a danger to our national interests as strong states." In short, there are plenty of statements by the majority party that would suggest bringing *Bikes and Bandages* to Afghanistan is not a partisan issue. Moreover, as your success in the Caribbean did not require any federal assistance, expanding these efforts to Afghanistan should be perceived as a win-win, even by fiscal conservatives.

---

[15] DC delegations differ tremendously. Whether the two senators from your state are in the same party or not, there will likely be some rivalry between them. Communications between the House and Senate are likely to be sporadic. Keep this in mind if you are attempting to coordinate an effort among Members within your DC delegation. Make sure you provide the same information to all contacts each time, because it is highly unlikely that the contacts involved are communicating regularly about your issue.

If the Member has a track record that makes you think she is unlikely to be supportive of your approach in general, is it possible to break down the issue into distinct pieces, humanize it, and find the hook that will bring the Member on board little by little? Is your friend in the National Guard willing to meet with Members and talk about her personal experience in Afghanistan? Remember that all of the folks in your community working on the project are also (hopefully) voting constituents who bring their own networks and possible connections to the Member. In both of the case studies listed, it would be well worth your effort to work with people who are already close to the Members, such as volunteers, campaign contributors, or people in the Member's social network.

Given its short attention span and domestic focus, Congress presents a challenge to those hoping to educate on broad and long-term security threats. Convincing your Member that diffuse, long-term projects that contribute to our nation's application of soft power most likely presents a challenge. This is why your discussion with a Member must couch the issue at hand in a broad understanding of security. Remember that you want to provide her with an opportunity to do something for you beyond merely voting your favor. Inviting the Member into a mutually beneficial relationship is your goal.

Initiating the Relationship

For example, consider the following fictitious conversation about international exchange programs:

> *You*: Mr. Representative, I'd like to tell you about a sister-cities program that Middletown has set up with the former Soviet republic of Uzbekistan. We organized this group after September 11th with the hope that Middle America could contribute to US security by educating itself and helping people around the world understand US culture and values.
>
> *Representative*: That's wonderful. Exposing cultures to each other is important, as is spreading American values.

You: We also would like to point out that now is a particularly important time for us to be involved. Uzbekistan is in the midst of a democratic transition from its Cold War past. Its institutions are fragile and our program specifically targets and supports young citizens— those who will make important decisions in ten years' time.

Representative: I agree with you. Attracting a young audience is very important for these efforts. The older leaders sometimes get stuck in their ways.

You: We tend to agree. That's why we hope you will consider our program part of a much broader, long-term security strategy for our country. Investments in citizen exchange are paying off. Just last year a former exchange student from the Republic of Georgia—who attended Columbia Law School—was elected president of his country. This is a tremendous achievement in view of the fact that Georgia used to be part of the Soviet Union. It is a fledgling democracy in a volatile part of the world. We now have a good friend in power and that can only help us.

Representative: That is very encouraging indeed.

You: Would you be willing to learn more about our program? We have a delegation coming in a few months. Perhaps we could organize an event at the library in Middletown and you could introduce our visitors.

Representative: I'll have to check my schedule…but it sounds good!

You: If that doesn't fit into your schedule, we could easily arrange for you to meet the three Uzbek high school exchange students living with Middletown families during one of the district recesses…

In this example, you framed international exchanges within the context of a security concern in simple, concise language and made a case for continued investment in light of evident returns. This fictitious discussion illustrates perfectly how soft security issue like people-to-people programs dovetails with a hard security concern like regional stability. It is also an example of how constituents can solicit Members' interest in a soft power element of the toolbox through a tangible local activity with a broader impact on the community. Through numerous interactions of this nature you will develop an ongoing relationship and become part of the Member's core constituent group. You will also have reference points and a healthy and trusting past relationship so that if an event does come up suddenly—perhaps Uzbekistan elects a new Western-oriented president who attended Middletown University—you will be able to respond quickly. Direct engagement to elicit the Member's awareness and an opportunity to build a trusting relationship can go a long way in overcoming outdated perceptions.

Members and Their Roles

Voting on legislation is only one of many roles played by our congressional leaders. According to Lee Hamilton, who served in Congress from 1965 to 1999, a "Help Wanted" ad for the job of congressman might read something like this:

> Wanted: Person with wide-ranging knowledge of scores of complex public policy issues. Must be willing to work long hours in Washington, then fly home to attend an unending string of community events. Applicant should expect that work and travel demands will strain family life, and that every facet of public and private life will be subject to intense scrutiny and criticism. [16]

According to Hamilton, Members typically perform the following roles:

- *national legislator* working to pass the laws of our nation and determine spending levels for thousands of federal programs;

- *local representative* serving the priorities, interests, and economic needs of the constituents;

---

[16] Hamilton, *How Congress Works and Why You Should Care*, p. 49.

- *constituent advocate* for individuals, groups, industries, and communities in the district;

- *committee member*, which requires developing specific expertise;

- *investigator* charged with oversight of the federal government;

- *educator* who can translate the work of Congress for constituents as well as the media;

- *student* of his or her constituents;[17]

- *local dignitary* performing ceremonial functions at home and serving as "ambassador" from the nation's capital;

- *fundraiser* in order to run for re-election;

- *staff manager* for anywhere between seventeen and eighty staffers in DC and at home;

- *party leader* in the party's caucus; and, lastly,

- a consummate *consensus builder*—both within and between parties.

The wide-ranging knowledge criterion in this job description inevitably implies assistance from many others, especially for Members with little to no previous experience or direct exposure to peace and security concerns. This is where a knowledgeable constituent or local organization can help. Again, try to think like a Member. What are the local issues that may relate to your Member's top priorities? Do any of the local issues provide a link to the activities of your organization or institution?

---

[17] Congressman Hamilton notes: "No matter what subject, there was always a constituent who knew more about it than I did." See Hamilton, p. 51.

For our purposes, the Member's role as legislator, representative, constituent advocate, educator, and student all suggest the breadth of opportunities for an engaged constituency. In an ideal situation, the engaged constituent or local organization can help educate the Member or his staffer. As suggested by our case study, with the Member as newly minted expert on conflict resolution, the Member can then serve as an *educator* to others in the district or his colleagues in Congress. As a *constituent advocate* the Member should be perceived as a part of your coalition. As opinion leaders in their district, state, and nation, Members can, at times, help organize constituent interests back at home to create an even broader coalition of support. Do not overlook any of these roles in seeking to educate Members or to get them to work with you on educating their colleagues and the public at large. The roles played by a Member might be critically important to the growth of conflict resolution programs and recognition of their contribution to remedying US security concerns. Similarly, such a coalition might be necessary for successfully expanding the *Bikes and Bandages* effort to Afghanistan, in light of additional transportation costs, security concerns, and more extensive cultural barriers.

Members and the Media

Members of Congress regard press relations as vital. Almost every office has a press secretary (or communications director) whose job usually encompasses handling the Member's relations with the media, writing press releases regarding the Member's actions or opinions, and analyzing and monitoring local events to see if actions taking place in DC can get good press coverage for the Member. The press secretary is also responsible for collecting, compiling, and disseminating the headline articles from major national newspapers—as well as any articles mentioning the Member by name, whether in a national, regional, or local newspaper—to everyone on the Member's staff daily. The articles compiled are not just from print media but also include online resources of different varieties. People on the Hill are deluged continuously with headlines and have little to no time to decipher and synthesize the information received. This relates to the next chapter on the importance of turning information into knowledge, but it also underscores how the media plays a major role in the lives of our elected leaders (and their staffs). Getting favorable coverage of a Member's activities or positions on an issue is a fundamental motivating factor as a measure of job performance, not just for the press secretary but also for the other staffers advising the Member.[18]

Good press relations are not just a convenience. The effectiveness of a Member's relations with the press will sometimes determine the success of many of his other activities, such as promoting his position or legislation. The media also serve as a critical link to the larger political environment and a source for different ideas, recommendations, views, and reactions. Conversely, the press is also a political tool through which a Member can communicate his views and objectives directly to people. If a Member is a lousy communicator, his re-election prospects may be threatened. Losing touch with the desires of constituents and local issues and failing to communicate with those same constituents via the media, are paths to defeat. For this reason reporters readily gain access to lawmakers. Regardless of occasional animosity and wariness between them, the symbiotic relationship between the journalist and the legislator is fundamental to the democratic process.[19] The action-reaction feedback loops among the public, the media, and our elected leaders must be seen as a complex whole.

The activist and educator need to be attentive to the media as a useful tool in promoting their causes. Members of Congress are extremely sensitive to the press, even "Letters to the Editor." When appropriate, the activist should seek to get press for her issue or event and then use that press coverage to interest the Member. Activists can use the "hook" of positive press coverage for an event to compel a Member to participate. Remember also that local and national press has varying levels of significance. As one House Press Secretary said, "A representative lives and dies by the coverage of the hometown rag." While this is true for senators as

---

[18] Hill offices differ with respect to whom is allowed to talk to the media. In some instances, interaction with the media is solely handled by the press secretary, while in others, more senior staffers with expertise in a specific issue area are allowed latitude to interact with the press.

[19] For a summary of the reasons that media are crucial to Congress, see Silverberg, *Congress for Dummies*, p. 218.

well, a Senate office will be concerned about local, regional, and even national coverage.

Let us turn to our case studies as they apply to the possible role of media.

CASE STUDY ONE: PEACE AND CONFLICT STUDIES

Will you be holding a conference to which you can invite the Member to offer a keynote speech? Can you get press involved and portray the Member in a positive light? Does the Member have someone on staff willing to talk to your class about the role of conflict prevention in US foreign policy? Has the Member done anything recently on peace and security issues about which you could write a supportive op-ed or "Letter to the Editor?" Are there local legislators with an interest who could also participate? The media can be the initial hook to get the Member's interest. They can be leveraged for an event in which the Member has agreed to take part. And they can be used as an educational tool by people in the program or by your Member as part of the coalition.

CASE STUDY TWO: BIKES AND BANDAGES ABROAD

Similar thinking applies to this case. Could you interest a local journalist in writing an article about *Bikes and Bandages* for the local newspaper? Is there an opportunity to mention the expansion of *Bikes and Bandages* to Afghanistan and underscore women's rights as part of your educational strategy for young girls to elicit your Member's support? Can you involve both the Member and local media in an event at the high school to recognize the public service contributions made by the nurse and students in this effort? Any or all of these possibilities can leverage the media to get the Member's attention. If the Member is involved in an event, remember "above all" that your goal is to have the Member portrayed in a positive light.

CONCLUSION

Although Congress is a stimulus-response institution, pressure is not the only way to get a Member to respond. Hard-and-fast realities are reflected in party loyalties, political constraints, and committee assignments. In addition, relationships matter. A good lobbyist knows that Members of Congress respond to their friends.

Thus, he will devote his energies to building those relationships and then use those relationships to strategize about the best ways to move his issues forward. An engaged and informed constituency should do the same. When meeting with a Member or staffer, or when seeking to get a Member to speak to your group, try to think like a Member. What knowledge or resources might you bring to bear that are useful to the Member? How can his involvement in this issue benefit him and his constituents? Is it an issue the Member can take to his colleagues in Congress? Can he make a name for himself, carving out an area of special expertise and providing leadership? Is it something he will feel good about working on?

The constituency basis of American politics offers a key way of providing alternative views and influencing Members' willingness to spend political capital. There are many creative ways to offer support to a Member, and, in turn, to reap benefits from his increased attention to your issue. Too often, public interest advocates fail to notice the extent to which Members of Congress appreciate the support of knowledgeable people, especially from their own district or state, who are willing to engage them in meaningful activities. Your goal should be to become part of the Member's key constituent groups whose resources—knowledge, local activities, access to means of communication and organizational skills—he finds useful. At the same time, Members of Congress have organizing resources at their disposal. If you can get one or more Members to buy into an idea, they can help you educate others, both in Congress and at home. Is it possible to think of your Member as part of the coalition? This prospect opens the door for leveraging the Members' access and reach in order to expand your coalition. Lastly, understanding the various roles Members perform, as well as how the media figures into each role, will be an important part of your strategy.

4

Turning Information Into Knowledge

A nyone interested in providing his knowledge to an audience on Capitol Hill must first do a bit of homework to ensure that his outreach efforts get the right information into the most important hands. In the preceding chapter, we discussed some of the general parameters within which each Member operates, the numerous roles Members perform, and the use of the media as part of the strategy. In this chapter, we will address the tactical basics for packaging your message and approaching the Hill. We will outline a general description of the foreign and security policy landscape in Congress, and provide insights into issue-specific power dynamics and structural deficiencies of the institution. This information will give you a better understanding of how Congress works so that you will be able to devise an effective strategy for outreach to representatives and senators.[1]

In order to clarify general aspects of institutional structures, we will again use two fictional examples. The following case studies of security issues—the first on biodefense and public health, the second on advancing civil society in Liberia—will introduce you to potential audiences on the Hill.

CASE STUDY ONE: BIODEFENSE AND PUBLIC HEALTH

The Institute for Smarter Policy (ISP) has been collaborating with the Association of Ivory Towers (AIT) and several US agencies on a project to address biodefense. Their focus is public health infrastructure and its response capabilities as measured against a mandate from a federal program called Project Bioshield. Over a one-year period, two senior researchers at ISP and members of AIT have directed a research project involving representatives from the Department of Homeland Security (DHS), the Centers for Disease Control (CDC), and their counterparts at the National

---

[1] Tips and tools for legislative research, as well as advice on avoiding political "third rails," will be addressed later in Chapter 4.

Institute for Allergic and Infectious Disease (NIAID). Several biomedical experts from the private sector were also consulted. The objectives of this effort were to:

- assess whether the Next-Generation Medical Countermeasures program sufficiently funded therapeutic treatments, as opposed to vaccines;[2]

- measure progress made within the National Institute of Health's (NIH) efforts to speed research and development on Medical Countermeasures;

- determine how the Food and Drug Administration (FDA) was proceeding with possible Emergency Use Authorization for newly developed medical countermeasures;

- evaluate whether funding was allocated according to a reasonable assessment of threats both from human-induced and naturally occurring infectious diseases in order to maximize the "dual-use" potential of the funding;

- identify gaps in interagency and public-private coordination for responding to a successful terrorist attack or to an outbreak of a highly virulent and contagious infectious disease; and

- offer recommendations to increase the effectiveness of federal funding and response capacity among federal, state, local, and private-sector actors.

The product of this study is a 350-page report and an additional ninety-four pages of tables and appendices. The report's executive

---

[2] A therapeutic countermeasure would be any treatment (including a vaccine) given to people already exposed to a biological agent in order to prevent or ameliorate disease, while a preventive vaccine would be administered to an unexposed–but presumably vulnerable–population for the same purpose. These choices between a subgroup and an entire population point to dramatically different costs and implementation plans of a program.

summary totals eleven pages and describes the methodology used by the project, lists the findings along with specific examples, and outlines recommendations to improve the program's effectiveness. The report goes into extensive detail regarding the amounts of funding allocated to specific endeavors for the Next-Generation Medical Countermeasures program. The report elaborates possible research on therapeutic countermeasures that are receiving very little or no funding under the program. The findings indicate that no assessment of the overlap between threats of emerging infectious disease and possible terrorist threats was done prior to allocation of the funds. Moreover, very little threat assessment went into prioritizing the funding of research to counter terrorist threats. Vaccines were given much higher priority than funding for therapeutic countermeasures. In addition, substantial coordination gaps were identified among the federal agencies and public- and private-sector actors that could facilitate a rapid response to a health crisis.

How do you present the findings and recommendations of this detailed report to Congress? Which Members of Congress and which committees should be included in an outreach effort to increase awareness of these findings and recommendations?

CASE STUDY TWO: ADVANCING CIVIL SOCIETY IN LIBERIA

The nongovernmental, not-for-profit humanitarian organization Human Security First (HSF) works as a subcontractor to the US Agency for International Development (USAID) on projects to build civil-society and promote free media in Liberia. HSF has been operating "on the ground" in Liberia since the election of Charles Taylor as President in 1997. Although representatives of HSF had to leave Liberia during the civil conflict that erupted in 2003, the stabilization of Liberia through the efforts of the Economic Community of West African States (ECOWAS) and the UN made sufficient progress in the last months of 2003 to allow nongovernmental organizations to return to the country and begin rebuilding.

HSF did not receive any of the $400 million allocated for Liberia in the emergency supplemental legislation passed by Congress in 2003. However, HSF successfully bid on a USAID contract for development efforts in Liberia from fiscal year 2004 international operations funding. With initial funding from

USAID of $200,000, HSF was able to launch three radio stations now almost entirely staffed by Liberians. HSF has also moved forward in its efforts to establish a human rights monitoring network in several areas of the country. Depending on future funding from USAID, HSF believes that an important next step in Liberia's development would be to increase the availability of primary education, especially outside the capital, Monrovia. How can HSF's Washington office work to educate Hill staff about its work and its relevance to US interests in Liberia and West Africa?

WHAT IS APPROPRIATE TO BRING TO THE HILL?

A 400-page philosophical volume on human rights and humanitarian intervention is probably not an appropriate educational tool for a Capitol Hill audience, unless it directly relates to a current question on the minds of policymakers. Even if an example of US humanitarian intervention is regularly in the headlines, translating the major findings to the specific case at hand would be necessary in order for the topic to garner any interest. For example, let us assume that the above research findings indicate that early intervention saved lives, decreased the likelihood of future human rights abuses, and made reconciliation between perpetrators and victims more readily feasible. Could these findings be applied to a timely example of US intervention? Is there an available "lessons-learned" report on a recent case of intervention that would provide a helpful contrast to other episodes throughout history? If so, a Capitol Hill audience might be enticed into understanding the relevance of the work to the policymaking process.

Think tanks and academic organizations spend a great deal of money producing hundreds of glossy publications to distribute across Capitol Hill. With rare exceptions, these reports get tossed away or stashed in bookcases without ever being reviewed. In a best-case scenario, the executive summary is skimmed by the appropriate staffer and the report finds its way into the garbage can. The fact is that very few staffers will understand the nuances of the subject at hand, and even fewer will have the time to wade through a lengthy report. One staffer even made the suggestion to "tell those groups to stop sending up 535 glossy, expensive reports and spend the money on an outreach coordinator instead!" Even a ten-page executive summary requires a greater time commitment than most staffers can afford.

Focus on "Action Items" and Recommendations

Despite the disparate nature of the two cases described at the beginning of this section, both contain information that could be highly relevant to policymakers on the Hill. Whereas the biodefense report in its entirety is of less use, the findings and recommendations included in that report may prove highly useful to congressional policy decisions about the structure and focus of the program, as well as future funding allocations. The study's authors should carefully extract the findings and recommendations that Congress can influence, and package them in a fact sheet using the most straightforward and simple language possible. Ideally, a briefing held on Capitol Hill for interested staffers would offer an additional opportunity to convey the study's main points and offer clear recommendations for possible congressional actions on the structure of the programs and corresponding funding. The briefing, along with a summary of findings and recommendations, allows staffers to have the most important content at their disposal and to discuss the main points of the paper with the foremost experts in the field. In this manner, the briefing and the fact sheet provide conduits for getting critical knowledge into the hands of relevant policymakers.

The Liberia case is entirely different from the biodefense case due to the nature of the activity and the security concerns it addresses. But the basics remain the same. HSF should not devote tremendous resources to compiling a report on its work in Liberia; however, a one-page fact sheet about the funding received and concrete progress made on the ground with US taxpayer moneys can make a compelling case without being a "lobbying" effort. In addition, as with the biodefense case, a forum including a representative from HSF who has been working in Liberia, along with a USAID counterpart, would provide a similar opportunity for conveying the success and importance of these activities to Congress.

In both cases, the following rules apply:

- A brief fact sheet (two pages at a maximum) with direct relevance to Congress' role is a good tool.

- An opportunity to brief Members or staffers can significantly enhance Congress' understanding and interest in the subject.

- For any briefing, select persons who are articulate and concise, and who know the political landscape surrounding the issue.

- Get bipartisan support for the briefing in order to increase participation and get maximum buy-in at the outset.

- Representatives from federal agencies, especially those who have been on the ground implementing the policy (and spending the money), should be part of any panel for the briefing. This makes the link to Congress explicit and the views offered more readily accepted.

- Consider offering food.[3] Ask yourself whom you want to attend. If you want to cast the net wide for a general education effort, be prepared to buy lunch for lots of interns. You just might draw in a few interested staffers as well. It has been our experience that the staffers who are dedicated to the issue come whether or not food is offered.

- If possible, organize constituent pressure. Make sure that like-minded membership-based organizations are aware of this educational opportunity and ask them to alert their members across the country. A staffer who receives twenty emails from constituents about the importance of an upcoming briefing will be much more likely to attend.

Congressional Committees

The committee structure on Capitol Hill, unfortunately, does not coexist well with the demands of today's domestic and

---

[3] Members of Congress may not sponsor food-events directly. Members can endorse the events, but your organization will have to send out the initial notification, and you must work directly with the Special Events and Catering Office.

international security environments. With the exception of the changes to accommodate the creation of the Department of Homeland Security in 2003, the committee structures in Congress for foreign and security policymaking have not undergone a comprehensive adaptation to reflect the end of the Cold War. Despite the fact that September 11th demonstrated quite clearly that US security concerns transcend institutions that were established for a different era, very little has changed in Congress to adapt the committee structure in order to achieve coherent and balanced security policy.

As mentioned in Chapter 2, Congress has two fundamental responsibilities in policymaking: authorizing and appropriating. Committees that actually set policy are known as *authorization* committees. *Appropriations* committees, on the other hand, are responsible for a detailed allocation of funding according to the budget resolution. The Appropriations Committees in both the House and the Senate are divided into thirteen subcommittees, and each subcommittee must pass a bill each year allocating specific funding amounts for the agencies under its jurisdiction.[4] The defense account (the so-called "050" budget) receives oversight scrutiny via annual authorization and appropriations bills, each of which is brought to the floor, debated, amended, and passed by the entire chamber. Defense programs authorized in the defense authorization bill are more specifically allocated by the Defense, Military Construction, and Energy and Water Appropriations Subcommittees.[5]

The soft power equivalent to the 050 defense account is the so-called Function 150 "Foreign Operations" Account; this account includes funding for State Department operations and US foreign assistance, allocated by the Commerce-Justice-State and Foreign Operations Appropriations Subcommittees respectively. Although annual appropriations apply to all discretionary accounts of US

---

[4] See Chapter 3 for further explanation of the budget process. Also see House Budget Committee, *The Congressional Budget Process: An Explanation*, 105th Cong., 2nd sess., revised 1998, available online at http://www.house.gov/budget_democrats_/budget_process/_budget_process.pdf_ and *Compilation of Laws and Rules Relating to the Congressional Budget Process*, available online at http://www.house.gov/budget_democrats/budget_process/budget_laws.pdf.

[5] For a detailed analysis of the defense budget process, see Mary T. Tyszkiewicz and Stephen Daggett, *A Defense Budget Primer,* Congressional Research Service report RL30002, December 9, 1998.

foreign policy agencies as well, one significant difference persists in the authorization and appropriations cycle. The policy-setting process via authorization legislation, especially debate by the full House or Senate, occurs less frequently for the non-defense instruments of US national power as will be discussed in more detail below.

Regardless of the program under consideration, though, if the program is authorized, but not appropriated, the authorization language for the program amounts to a "hollow" budget item and the program most likely will not get started or continue. If the money is appropriated, but not authorized, the program is highly likely to move forward. In other words, when Congress appropriates money for a specific use by an agency, the agency will in turn spend the money for that purpose. The inverse does not hold true: If Congress authorizes a program, but the agency does not receive money to fund that program, then the authorization amounts to an "unfunded mandate." This latter scenario is further exacerbated by the drift of power and influence from authorization to appropriations committees, as we noted earlier. In short, too often money makes policy.

The relative importance of authorization and appropriations committees is perhaps seen most clearly in the realm of security and foreign policymaking. This characteristic is reflected in the history of US foreign assistance legislation. The last time Congress enacted a comprehensive foreign aid authorization bill, articulating new strategic objectives and outlining clear policies and priorities to attain those objectives, was 1985.[6] As such, for almost twenty years the Foreign Operations appropriations legislation has been the vehicle for not only allocating funding, but also modifying aid policy and attaching conditions to executive branch activities. Thus, with the notable exception of the Bush Administration's creation of the Millennium Challenge Account and congressional authorization of this initiative in 2003, "[i]t has been largely through Foreign Operations appropriations that the United States has modified aid policy and resource allocation

---

[6] Susan B. Epstein, *Foreign Relations Authorization, FY2004 and FY2005: An Overview*, Congressional Research Service Report RL31986, July 21, 2003, p. 1.

priorities since the end of the Cold War."[7]   This reality demonstrates the shift in authority from policy to money committees and the diminished congressional interest in foreign affairs during the 1990s.

Security Issues and Congressional Structures: A Mismatch

Our two case studies underscore one specific aspect of the organizational structure on Capitol Hill. While there would be little to no overlap in the *committee* staff interested in both the biodefense report and efforts to build a civil society in Liberia, many staffers in the *personal* offices of Members of Congress could use the information provided by both of these outreach efforts. Why? Because one person usually handles both defense and foreign policy issues in a Member's personal office. Moreover, most staffers who have the defense and/or foreign policy portfolio have probably also assumed responsibility for terrorism and homeland security. The benefits of covering the bases on both committee and personal staffs are well worth the time and effort, especially if you connect with the one staffer who is devoted to your issue.

CASE STUDY ONE: BIODEFENSE AND PUBLIC HEALTH

In this example, the committees of interest would be the authorization and appropriations subcommittees that have oversight responsibilities for homeland security, health, foreign relations, and defense. In addition to the Select Committee for Homeland Security, two other authorizing committees can assert jurisdiction over issues involving terrorism (i.e., the Subcommittee on International Operations and Terrorism under the Foreign Relations Committee, as well as the Subcommittee on Financial Management, the Budget, and International Security under the Government Affairs Committee). A recent structural change to the Armed Services Committee created a Subcommittee for Emerging Threats, which arguably also has oversight of terrorism as an emerging (or now fully emerged) threat.   The appropriations subcommittees that have oversight of biodefense efforts would

---

[7] Larry Nowels, *Appropriations for FY2004: Foreign Operations, Export Financing, and Related Programs*, Congressional Research Service Report RL31811, July 24, 2003, p. 3.

include Labor-Health and Human Services (Labor-HHS), Homeland Security, Commerce-Justice-State, and Foreign Operations. Many of the above committees can assert jurisdiction over biodefense or terrorism-preparedness initiatives, depending on the focus of the biological threat in question. Project Bioshield is largely funded by the Department of Health and Human Services or by an organization under its auspices. Therefore, your immediate target audience would likely be the staffers on the Health, Education, Labor, and Pensions (HELP) Committee and the corresponding appropriations clerks on the Labor-HHS Subcommittee under the Appropriations Committee.

While individuals affiliated with these two committees are the most likely targets of your findings and recommendations, the other committees mentioned should not be neglected in your outreach activities. Oftentimes something in a Member's personal or professional background will generate interests in areas that are not part of her role on a committee. Similarly, Members or staffers on a different committee with overlapping or parallel policy concerns are likely to take an interest in order to better understand the issues involved, because particular policy features do, in fact, frequently fall within their committee's jurisdiction. A narrow assessment of the committees with jurisdiction is not always the route to finding champions for your cause. For example, the House directory lists a Congressional Biomedical Research Caucus, as well as a House Biotechnology Caucus. Who belongs to these caucuses and what overlap, if any, do they have with committees of jurisdiction? Is the caucus relatively active and could it possibly help sponsor a briefing in the House to facilitate sharing of the report's recommendations?

Knowing which Members of Congress have played key roles in advancing your issue will be critical to the success of your approach. Researching your policy concern in order to determine who should be approached first is a fundamental step in deciphering the landscape and making wise choices in your allocation of time.

CASE STUDY TWO: ADVANCING CIVIL SOCIETY IN LIBERIA

As mentioned, the activities of HSF as a USAID subcontractor in Liberia should obviously be of direct interest to Members serving on the Senate Foreign Relations and House International

Relations Committees (especially on the Africa Subcommittees), as well as the Foreign Operations Appropriations Subcommittees. Yet it would be shortsighted to assume that only those Members (or their staffers) would take an interest. Can you find any Members (or staffers) who served in the Peace Corps? What about the Congressional Black Caucus or the Congressional Human Rights Caucus? While the caucus system was more active in earlier years when most had full-time staff, each caucus still lists a bipartisan group of Members who might be interested. Maybe a group of caucus members could spearhead the effort to inform Congress about HSF's activities.

ACCESS, PACKAGING, AND AUDIENCE

We return here to earlier themes of structural imbalances and outmoded perceptions by addressing how to get access, package your issue, and interact with a congressional audience. Just as "security" cannot be solely guaranteed by a better military with superior weapons, the entire spectrum of US engagement in the world consists of numerous activities beyond the Pentagon and the State Department. Problems of perceptions and priorities still exist in Congress as stubborn outgrowths of Cold War institutions and assumptions about the nature of "security." While commercial interests and their influence in the political process are one obstacle to fresh thinking, the problems extend further. To cite our case study example, there is no natural domestic constituency for initiatives focused on conflict prevention or civil society development in West Africa that parallel the existing or prospective defense jobs in a district.

The annual Pentagon budget ($400 billion) towers over all other forms of US engagement ($30 billion).[8] This thirteen-to-one budget ratio makes clear why defense issues are a much higher priority in Congress. The $400 billion amount cited covers all Pentagon spending, including non-discretionary personnel accounts, military construction at facilities throughout the world,

---

[8] These are rounded figures for the President's FY2005 budget request for defense, including nuclear activities in the Department of Energy budget, as opposed to the State Department and International Operations budgets. These figures do not include funds for the large emergency supplemental appropriations for Iraq and Afghanistan or for other activities at federal agencies that have an international component.

and the US nuclear weapons complex. The $30 billion purse is approximately what is allocated for State Department spending and US foreign operations. This figure includes all State Department costs (personnel, embassy construction, and security programs) as well as US bilateral assistance (Israel, Egypt, and Colombia receive the largest amounts), contributions to international financial institutions (the World Bank, the International Monetary Fund, and regional development banks), and USAID's programs worldwide.

As mentioned, the US military is increasingly involved in non-traditional missions throughout the world.[9] For example, Provisional Reconstruction Teams in Afghanistan represent a new effort to coordinate civil-military policy tools to provide Afghans with quick-turnaround reconstruction efforts like new schools and health clinics. Similarly, the nuclear weapons laboratories funded in the Department of Energy defense account are working on securing dangerous materials in the former Soviet Union and providing commercial opportunities for former Soviet weapons scientists. Despite these examples of defense-account allocations for non-traditional activities, such programs constitute such a small proportion of the defense account that the thirteen-to-one ratio is still valid.

Agenda and Access

What is the significance of this ratio in the daily agenda on Capitol Hill? Most staffers on the Hill are under no obligation to take or return phone calls from anyone other than constituents. So, if the area code is not from the home district or state, a typical outreach effort might fail with the first phone call. However, a defense and foreign policy staffer who gets a call from a lobbyist at Boeing or Lockheed Martin at a 703 area code (Virginia) will most likely return the phone call, even if there does not appear to be any direct connection to his district. The staffer's operating assumption would be that the lobbyist wants to talk about Air Force tankers or the Joint Strike Fighter program, or perhaps something that may come up for a vote during the floor debate on a

---

[9] There is an ongoing debate within the foreign and security policy community and within Congress about the appropriate civilian-military "division of labor." See www.effectivepeacekeeping.org or www.cgdev.org for more information.

bill. Or he may want to discuss a deal to bring jobs to the district. The staffer must ensure that his Member is not blindsided by an issue. Any or all of the above would be reason enough to return the phone call and assess whether anything beyond a short conversation is necessary.

Due to the stakes involved, defense lobbyists from major companies usually get their phone calls returned. The same would not necessarily hold true for the National Association of Conflict Resolution Practitioners (NACRP), unless the caller is also a constituent or has an established rapport with the office. If that constituent and member of the NACRP also happens to chair the local chapter of the American Bar Association (ABA) and is a professor at the university law school, getting a foot in the door on the Hill begins to look increasingly likely. (Every obvious tie this person has to organizations comprised of constituents will help.)

Being a constituent is usually sufficient to get a return phone call or a one-on-one meeting with the Member and/or staffer. Some tips for good meetings with Members and staffers can be found below. Consider whether or not contact with the Member is necessary, especially at the very beginning of the process. A first indication that someone truly does not understand Capitol Hill (or is simply self-important) is the degree to which he ignores or denigrates the young, eager staffer. Insistence on talking directly to the Member may be counterproductive in some cases. In many offices, the staffer is the subject matter expert and rarely requires the Member's direct intervention to have an influence on the policymaking process.

Access to committee staff is a different story. A committee staffer is generally less accessible and does not serve "constituents" in the same manner that a personal office staffer does. A committee staffer is responsive to the Members (and their staffs) who serve on the committee, and is responsible for oversight of the agencies under the committee's jurisdiction. However, if the issue at hand is a priority for the White House or the committee chairman or, say, the Majority Leader, getting access to a committee staffer is a good possibility. Another route would be to go through the personal office of a Member on that committee to try to get her help in making the introductions to committee staff.

These are just generalizations about how congressional offices and staffers function. With 535 Member offices on the Hill, you will probably find just as many variations on the theme. Some Members are hands-on about every issue and run horizontal organizations within their personal offices. Other offices will be more hierarchical, and staffers will have a bare minimum of "face time" with the Member. House staffers generally get more time with their Members, as there are fewer people in a personal office; at the same time, House staffers usually have more areas in their portfolios than their counterparts in the Senate, and thus less time to develop extensive expertise in an area. It is reasonably safe to say that from House to Senate, offices become more hierarchical and Members less accessible.

To sum up: A staffer who returns phone calls, cares about your issue, and is willing to put in a few extra hours for your cause can be worth his weight in gold. A staffer's investment usually reflects the Member's own interests, but that does not necessarily have to be the case. Sometimes staffers take personal initiative on issues that they care about.

Packaging Your Issue

Arguments for investments in security-related hardware, such as fighter jets, usually do not reach the same breadth and complexity as, say, poverty reduction as a tool in curbing terrorism. Linking US security to secular education for girls in Pakistan, for example, is not obvious to everyone. Be specific and make the linkages concrete. You might argue that your issue is a post-September 11th security concern because the girls' education program you sponsor is alleviating desperation, helping the local economy, and therefore lessening the chances for radicalization of the population. This soft security approach gets at a long-term, hard security risk: terrorism and regional stability.

"Framing" is Critical[10]

Making complex issues simple is imperative. Time is a scarce resource for Members of Congress and their staffs. A good first impression and a short, concise explanation of your issue are vital. Knowing the larger context for your topic and understanding its

---

[10] See Chapter 6 for a deeper discussion of "framing."

intersection with political priorities will be a critical aspect of appropriately "framing" it for a congressional audience. The title of your memo or briefing can, in and of itself, be a death knell, regardless of the importance of the topic. On a more positive note, if you can couch your issue within big-picture themes and tie its relevance to an issue in the daily headlines, you greatly increase your chances of garnering broader interest. Most importantly, you must ensure that the presentation is straightforward, avoids jargon, and makes clear why a congressional audience should care and what Congress can do about it.

Beware of Partisan Divisions

Regardless of how pragmatic and non-political your topic may seem, there will probably be partisan divisions over it or partisan issues that relate to it. Understanding the political terrain surrounding the topic will be critical to your success in relaying the information to the broadest audience possible. As unfortunate as it may seem, certain people on Capitol Hill simply will not listen if they catch a whiff of something that is on "the wrong side" of the issue. The partisan divisions on a subject can usually be determined through news articles or an online search. A review of the *Congressional Record* online or the *Roll Call* or *The Hill* newspapers might also provide valuable insights.

Terminology Matters

Inherently related to partisan divisions, the political vocabulary of a given period has tremendous influence on how people view a topic. Several terms today have become associated with the political divisions themselves, and the use of those terms can trigger unnecessary antagonism. For example, "nation-building" was a negative term prior to the US wars in Afghanistan and Iraq. Rather than using the title "nation-building in Liberia" to describe your effort, you could use terms such as "post-conflict stabilization," "reconstruction," or "civil society building in Liberia" to remain in safe territory. Another example is "multilateralism," which is now construed negatively by some due to the charges of "unilateralism" on the part of the Bush Administration. Rather than "multilateralism," you could use "international cooperation" or "international coordination" to convey the same idea. Be aware of the political lexicon, and be creative in adapting your message to avoid unnecessary divisions.

Blurring the Line

Despite the fact that committee jurisdictions on Capitol Hill are very rigid, the line between hard and soft approaches to security has become increasingly blurred. It behooves anyone working in the domain of soft security to encourage the *further* blurring of that line in order to elicit interest from hard security staffers. Many items in the soft security domain have hard security implications. It is entirely appropriate and necessary to ensure that the "defense/security" staffers and their Members on the Hill are getting sufficient information on the non-hardware components of a well-stocked toolkit. Inevitably, the tools of soft power have long-term benefits and are usually less costly than those implemented by the barrel of a gun. Many Members of Congress recognize the value of these tools; in fact, it is probably safe to suggest that a majority does. But advocating the soft tools goes against parochial interests, Cold War structural deficiencies, and an electorate that still perceives Pentagon spending as directly proportionate to US security. In local organizing terms, these perceptions are why it is so important for veterans and those with military experience to be included in outreach efforts. A Gulf War veteran or a retired four-star general advocating for more international cooperation makes a different kind of impression than "the usual peacenik suspects."

Who Will Oppose You?

As mentioned, you must do considerable research to identify which Members are potential allies. But just as much research should be devoted to Members "opposed" to your cause or who might have concerns about your objectives. The "opposed" is in quotations because it often has more to do with terminology or means than with the ultimate objectives. An allergic reaction to seemingly common-sense solutions might owe to something only an insider could detect, like the latest talking points memo from the party leadership.

The political terrain surrounding an issue matters. Terminology defines the path forward. If you can avoid raising red flags at the beginning, you can greatly ease the process of facilitating consensus down the road.

WARNING: At times, certain issues become toxic for a congressional audience because of the larger political discourse. In such cases, the facts simply do not matter and attempts at facilitating a constructive, bipartisan dialogue on Capitol Hill will, at best, be heard on only one side of the aisle. For example, as of this writing, issues such as military "preemption" against adversaries armed with weapons of mass destruction, the Comprehensive Test Ban Treaty, and the International Criminal Court (ICC) cannot be readily incorporated into a successful nonpartisan education campaign. Depending on your focus, the politics may suggest that sometimes there is *no bipartisan point of departure* to discuss an issue at hand. In such instances, talks with individual Members sympathetic to the cause are probably the only viable approach.

Hurt feelings and high-stakes politics on certain issues will ease over time, and opportunities for a balanced dialogue may surface in the future. For example, the Bush Administration's rejection of the Kyoto Treaty in 2001 created a temporary vacuum in Congress in the general areas of energy security, economics, and the environment. "Climate change" was a non-starter. But then, in October 2003, the bipartisan McCain-Lieberman bill (called the Climate Stewardship Act) was introduced. Although it was defeated 55-43, it signaled a shift in Congress' willingness to work constructively on this issue.

Let's return to our case studies to see how this guidance might apply.

CASE STUDY ONE: BIODEFENSE AND PUBLIC HEALTH

Biodefense issues are too new to have clearly defined and/or divisive political parameters. At this point, broad bipartisan agreement can be found: The threat looms and we must actively pursue the means to address it. However, there is division over the appropriate policies for international efforts. One absolute "third rail" in the arena of biological threats is the Biological Weapons Convention (BWC). In 2001, the Bush Administration rejected the most recent internationally negotiated verification protocol to this convention, and hence partisan emotions over BWC verification run high. You should therefore craft any approaches either as completely separate from, or as a necessary complement to, any eventual arms control agreement on biotechnology and biological weapons control. This approach will bypass the current "red flag" of partisan divisions on the issue. In addition, you should carefully research who introduced and cosponsored the legislation on Project Bioshield, any amendments offered to the bill, and floor statements included in the *Congressional Record* when it was passed in both the House and Senate.

CASE STUDY TWO: ADVANCING CIVIL SOCIETY IN LIBERIA

While historic ties and "US interest/obligation" may be compelling for some Members and staffers, it is Liberia's effect on West African stability that would appear more generally compelling. In other words, only an eclectic group of lawmakers might care enough about any individual country in Africa to champion a related cause. However, if the fate of that nation can be tied to larger regional or continental interests, a more solid case can be made.

In general, when international problems can be shown to be destabilizing for an entire region or threatening to obvious US interests, it is easier to garner attention for the cause. For example, what can be learned from peacekeeping efforts in Sierra Leone that might apply to Liberia? Which elements of the UN's planning in the mid-1990s must be avoided to prevent a future cycle of violence in Liberia?

WHO IS YOUR AUDIENCE? WHY SHOULD THEY CARE?

No matter how self-evidently important your concern seems, there is absolutely no reason to assume that people in Congress rank it as a priority. The pace on Capitol Hill is excruciating. Members and their staffers are stretched thin, and time is often too short for them to gain much expertise on the numerous issues in their portfolios. Consider the twenty-five-year-old staffer whose portfolio includes defense, foreign policy, homeland security, and veteran's affairs. From September 2001 to January 2002 alone, the following events controlled his life and occupied his attention:

- the terrorist attacks on September 11th;
- war in Afghanistan;
- anthrax attacks on Capitol Hill;
- US withdrawal from the ABM Treaty; and
- the Bush Administration's 2002 Nuclear Posture Review.

Meanwhile, he was trying to ensure that all requested money for the district made its way into the defense appropriations bill, seeking opportunities to get money for his district from the emergency supplemental spending bill, and trying to track the deployments of local Guard and Reserve forces for Operation Noble Eagle[11] and Operation Enduring Freedom.[12] While those four months were particularly chaotic, this young man struggled everyday to gather enough understanding of a given event or executive decision to provide solid advice to his Member, craft good questions for hearings, and write accurate, astute floor statements for his Member on all of the above topics. All along he also had to respond promptly and appropriately to constituent inquiries.

Your typical House staffer in a personal office is in his mid-twenties, came to Capitol Hill straight from college, and was given a portfolio similar to the one listed above. His job performance is based on how well he serves his representative. The foremost priority is ensuring that his representative does not get blindsided by something. This requires him to remain adequately informed about issues in the district that fall within his portfolio–such as a change of command at the local base or a groundbreaking ceremony for a new counterterrorism center at the local university– and activities on the Hill that may jeopardize his representative's objectives.

---

[11] Operation Noble Eagle began the same day as the September 11th terrorist attacks with the deployment of active, reserve, and guard assets to secure, among a range of other things, US airspace and to patrol US airports.
[12] Operation Enduring Freedom began on October 7, 2001 with military strikes in Afghanistan to topple the Taliban regime and was still ongoing as of spring 2004.

Second, the staffer must ensure that constituents feel the representative's office is responsive to their concerns. This will entail numerous meetings with the people representing defense interests in the district (especially if his boss serves on one of the defense committees and there are contracting activities in the district), veterans' groups, self-proclaimed homeland security experts "with a better mousetrap," and so on. He may occasionally take a meeting with the local chapter of Amnesty International or an anti-nuclear organization. How this staffer allocates time will largely be a result of what his boss cares about—usually a product of committee assignments, and the pressures applied by constituents. As mentioned previously, constituents usually get their phone calls answered and can frequently get face-to-face meetings with staffers. Responsibilities for some constituent concerns—"casework"—and local events are usually carried by the representative's field office staff. However, the DC-based staffer must still be in touch with the field staff on high-profile issues in case the representative asks about them.

In short, the staffer in the House who covers foreign policy and/or defense often has four to six other issues to cover. The downside of these staffing responsibilities is that issues like foreign policy—issues that require extra, non-district specific work—often end up in the bottom of the inbox. The upside is that a friendly, well-organized, and informed constituent can become an influential asset if the representative decides to become more active on peace and security issues.

The Senate is a bit different. A Senate staffer often has a graduate degree or other life experience beyond Capitol Hill, and therefore is usually a bit older. His portfolio also tends to be somewhat smaller, because senators have larger staffs. It is important to remember, however, that his senator is responsible for a state, so there are more issues to track and a broader constituency to serve. The motivations for the Senate staffer parallel those of his House counterpart: serving the senator by being responsive to her interests and ensuring that constituents feel the senator's office is adequately attending to their concerns. In both the House and Senate, some offices will have fellows who specialize in foreign policy or defense issues. These fellows are often loaned or "detailed" from agencies or from academic organizations, and hence will enjoy the chance to discuss "big picture" issues.

Fellows, especially those detailed from agencies, are good initial contacts for any office.

The high turnover rate of staffers, especially in the House, inevitably affects outside groups' ability to have a consistent presence and build influence in any one office. It is therefore important to be aware of that turnover rate and to stay on top of it. It can also be seen as an opportunity, where the local organization serves as the institutional memory for the Member and her staff and regularly treks to the Hill for "get to know you" and "how can we help you?" meetings. Additionally, it may well serve your interest to keep track of staffers even after they leave the Hill. After all, they usually leave the Hill and enter academia, think tanks, agencies, or businesses where they could remain allies.

Committee versus Personal Staff

While one can say that age and experience generally increase from House to Senate, expertise increases dramatically from personal to committee staff in both chambers. Many committee staffers have lengthy track records on the Hill and start their careers in entry-level positions in personal offices, get promoted to legislative assistants, and then (usually) with the support of their Members land positions as professional staffers on committees. Senior committee staffers sometimes will also have held positions in the executive branch, taught at universities, or worked at policy research organizations. In short, committee staffers will usually be issue area experts with a great deal of substantive knowledge.

> **WARNING:** When meeting with a staffer on the Hill– whether from a personal or committee office and regardless of age–it is best not to assume anything about her level of knowledge on your issue. Sometimes that young female staffer with the defense and foreign policy portfolio also has a PhD in a relevant field or has served in the military, and you have to convince her of the validity of your idea or project before getting a chance to talk to the Member. Be respectful and do not condescend. Although young and perhaps not up-to-speed on your specific issue, most Hill staffers are quick learners and information sponges if they think the information is relevant to their job performance,

key to a current issue, or unique in its potential to make their Member a star.

Be Patient Yet Persistent

Many nuts-and-bolts jobs in Washington, DC, are staffed by interns. True to stereotype, answering phones is a typical job, both for interns and for junior staffers who are rapidly moving up the ladder. For this reason, the person who answers the phone at your Member's DC office might not know whom to go to in the office about your issue. Having something specific like a bill number of relevance to your interest or a narrow topic will help him ask around the office. Be patient.

FINDING A CHAMPION FOR YOUR CAUSE

The Right of First Refusal

For most topics, there will be Members who have some claim of ownership over certain issues based on their legislative track records. For example, Senator Pete Domenici (R-NM) has a longstanding record of leadership on mental health issues, and Congresswoman Lynn Woolsey (D-CA) is a well-known champion of international women's rights. As mentioned previously, you will want to make sure that you approach the most obvious Members first—those who have a history of working on the subject at hand—to give them the right of first refusal to discuss the topic and ways to increase congressional attention to it, help you with outreach on the Hill, or sponsor a briefing to discuss the topic.

The Unusual Suspects

You should also give some thought to the *unusual* suspects. By this we mean the Members who are not necessarily on the committee of jurisdiction for your issue, such as the Armed Services or Foreign Relations Committees, and who also are not necessarily in the party leadership. Sometimes a champion for your issue arises not because the Member serves on a specific committee, but rather due to a nexus with the Member's personal background. Was the Member in the Peace Corps? Does the Member have experience with a church missionary group? The personal is often political, even for our elected leaders. For example, former Senator and Majority Leader Robert Dole credited an Armenian doctor with saving his life during World War II. Senator Dole's office obviously became the first stop for any Armenian group seeking attention to its concern. It is important to remember that because Congress is a critical-mass organization—you never know when one vote will tip the scales—every single individual counts. For this reason, outreach to Members who are "unusual suspects" yields long-term benefits for international cooperative security.

Under the category of unusual suspects, you should approach new Members in particular. Often the Members most interested in working with outside groups on cooperative international issues are the newest Members of the House and Senate. New Members spend much of their first terms looking for ways to differentiate themselves from the pack. In addition, they are looking for issues that make them look more like leaders and that allow them to flaunt their credentials on a larger stage. Foreign policy and defense issues fit these criteria, as they allow Members to refer to the importance of the common good and to talk about concepts like peace and prosperity.

Let us return to our case studies in order to illustrate how this information about our audience applies.

CASE STUDY ONE: BIODEFENSE AND PUBLIC HEALTH

In the initial phone call to an office, it will be hard to know which staffer is the appropriate contact. It will probably be the person responsible for "homeland security," but it will be important to clarify whether or not the "health" staffer might instead be the right contact. For example, the homeland security staffer may deal mostly with local police and fire chiefs and with the federal moneys they receive for training. The medical response issues may get handled by a different staffer entirely, based on that staffer's exposure to "public health" issues. If a constituent played a role in this study, using that constituent as an intermediary is the best approach. If not, perhaps there is another link to the district, such as a medical research institute that receives funding from Project Bioshield. Of course, if your recommendations suggest that the type of funding that the local research institute receives is not the priority, you definitely do not want to use that conduit.

Perhaps a public health office in the district would take an interest and facilitate an introduction. Once the door is open, it is incumbent upon you to make a short, compelling case to the staffer (or Member) in order to garner the office's initial support or to request any assistance with additional outreach opportunities.

CASE STUDY TWO: ADVANCING CIVIL SOCIETY IN LIBERIA

As HSF's US headquarters are in Washington, its "constituent" status will not go very far. The same would largely apply to offices located in the Maryland or Virginia suburbs of Washington. A better route would be to identify those Members who have taken a particular interest in Liberia or West Africa in the past. Which Members supported the amendment for Liberia in the 2003 emergency supplemental? [13] A staffer in one of those offices will probably return your phone call and make time for a meeting based on his Member's interest. Which Members have taken an interest in Africa more generally? What about international education? Do they have an interest in peacekeeping or stability operations? Don't forget the caucuses mentioned previously. If HSF were based far outside the Beltway, then it would need to look carefully at what other options (both House and Senate) might be available for approaching the Hill. In the initial phone call to the Hill, finding the right staffer is less of a challenge. Ask to talk to the foreign policy staffer; this should land you at the right voicemail box.

BUILDING COALITIONS

Although it will take additional time at the outset, researching the policy institutes, advocacy organizations, or others with a link to your issue and then building a coalition to help with outreach can greatly enhance your impact down the road. Numerous organizations based inside the Beltway can become either partners or impediments. Most of these organizations will have some pre-greased connections to the Hill. Making the connections to other organizations with similar interests in a district, or inside the Beltway, can exponentially increase the network to Members on the Hill and the opportunities to affect the debate.

---

[13] For a discussion of emergency supplemental appropriations, see Chapter 5.

In order for our interests in peace and security to reach a critical mass of elected leaders, collaboration and information-sharing among concerned citizens is vital. When you are building your strategy, find "grasstops" or notable people who have some special influence (e.g., they went to college with the Member, they are an influential member of the community). These people have sway. Find them. Convince them. Get them engaged, even if in small ways. Also, consider giving a de-brief of your experience to other local groups, or write up your "lessons learned" and make them available online.

CONCLUSION

Both the biodefense study and capacity-building activities in Liberia fall under the umbrella of "security." However, the Members and staffers who will take an interest will differ dramatically. In both instances, producing useful knowledge for the right Member or staffer will require carefully thinking through the relevance of the information for a congressional audience, framing it to avoid partisan divisions, and making it simple enough for the outsider to readily comprehend. You must research the political landscape thoroughly in order to avoid potentially off-putting terminology, to decipher the connection to issues that Congress is currently considering, and to determine which offices to approach with your pitch. Using the examples outlined in this chapter as they apply to your own issue should help inform your approach and facilitate your success. (If you fall under certain lobbying restrictions, you will also need to pay particular attention to the rules as they apply in your case and tailor your approach accordingly.) All of these steps require an investment up front, but paying attention to these details will help ensure your success once you get past the intern and the voicemail box to a face-to-face meeting.

5

Nuts and Bolts

This chapter will help to provide additional information and resources for your organizing and outreach quest. Understanding the basics about the legislative process, particularly the budget process and its peculiarities, is essential to good timing and eventual success in your endeavor. Similarly, understanding the procedures, expectations, and methods common to Members of Congress, both in Washington and at home, will help you to better formulate your approach to engaging a Member or his staff and increasing your outreach potential.

LEARNING HOW CONGRESS WORKS

Rest assured, Congress remains confounding even to people who have worked on Capitol Hill for years. There will always be surprises and uncertainties regarding the political winds. But it still does not hurt to know the basics about the legislative process, and more specifically about how a bill becomes law. Some good basic information can be found in many volumes of work about the legislative process. Excellent, concise, and timely resources, many of which are available online, are also available from the Congressional Research Service (CRS).

Anyone wishing to educate Congress on an issue needs to have a general idea of the legislative process, a good sense of the appropriate timing for making the case, an understanding of the committee structure and what offices to approach first, as well as some comprehension of the budget process and the role of the Appropriations Committee in influencing policy. Cursory explanations of how a bill becomes law and the budget process follow.

How a Bill Becomes Law

First, any Member of Congress can introduce a piece of legislation. The proposed legislation is assigned a number and labeled with the name(s) of the sponsor(s). The bill is referred to the appropriate committee, usually based on the parliamentarian's assessment of which committee should have jurisdiction. Bills may be referred to more than one committee. For example, an energy policy bill introduced in the Senate that also addresses regulatory changes for the Environmental Protection Agency would most likely be referred to the Senate Energy and Natural Resources Committee, as well as the Committee on Environment and Public Works.

Typically, committee actions on legislation include asking for comments on the bill from government agencies, holding hearings, and convening a mark-up session to amend or provide additions to the bill prior to a "clean" bill being sent to the floor. (This new bill will have a different number than the original bill.) A committee chair may also fail to act on a bill, the equivalent of killing it; legislation "dies in committee" quite frequently.

When brought to the floor—which is not the inevitable outcome of passing a bill out of committee—the bill will be debated, possibly further amended, and then brought to a final up-or-down vote. In theory, any piece of legislation must go through the introduction, vetting by committee, and floor passage in both chambers. As noted in Chapter 2, however, overriding or circumventing the committee of jurisdiction is increasingly common. If the House and Senate pass identical bills, the agreed upon bill is then sent to the president. If the bills are different, then a conference committee must reconcile these differences, usually comprised of senior members of the committee that originally dealt with the bill. The conference report must be approved again by both the House and Senate.

Upon passage of a conference report by both chambers, the bill is sent to the president. A bill becomes law within ten days, when Congress is in session, if the president does not veto it. However, if Congress adjourns before the ten days have lapsed and the president does not sign the bill, it does not become law. (This is called a "pocket veto.") If the president vetoes the bill, both chambers must approve the bill by a two-thirds majority to override the president's veto. If a bill is signed or his veto is overridden, it becomes law.

The legislative process is simple in terms of the steps, but there are thousands of procedural rules, as well as political concerns, that influence the outcome at each step. For example, the Chairman of a committee may not allow committee consideration of a bill due to his own ideological beliefs, even though a majority of the committee members, as well as a majority in the chamber, would be in favor of the legislation. Similarly, a Senate Majority Leader may not prioritize bringing an item to the floor for Senate action, because the floor debate may offer an opportunity to make the White House look bad based on an issue that is getting a lot of public attention. These are but two examples of a vast range of reasons why a bill might get stalled or die a quiet death somewhere in the process.

One additional piece of information about this process is important. We are writing this handbook during the second session of the 108th Congress. A "new" Congress convenes every two years in the January following the November congressional elections. Typically, each Congress meets in two annual "sessions," one in its first calendar year and another in the second calendar year. Thus, the first session of the 109th Congress will occur in 2005 and the second session in 2006.

A bill introduced in February of the first session of a Congress remains "pending business" through the end of the second session of the Congress. At the beginning of the each Congress, the slate is wiped clean of all "pending" bills. Commonly, it will take more than one two-year Congress to get any legislation through the entire process of becoming a law, and Members will have to reintroduce any legislation that did not make it through at the beginning of the next Congress.

The Budget Process

On the first Monday of February each calendar year, the president sends to Congress his "blueprint" of the federal budget. This blueprint is the result of extensive interactions within each agency and between the individual agencies, the Office of Management and Budget (OMB), and the White House. The President's Budget (PB) outlines in great detail the priorities for spending and the exact funding for each agency and program under its auspices. While Congress "holds the purse strings," the president's priorities and outlines of allocations in this initial budget will continue to hold sway throughout the process. Initially, the House and Senate Budget Committees start work on a budget resolution, which is essentially a framework within which members will make decisions about funding allocations. In theory, a budget resolution, agreed upon by a conference committee, gets passed by both the House and Senate, providing an outline for the Appropriations Committee to follow with respect to funding allocations. The budget resolution is not a law and does not need to be signed by the president; it is merely guidance for the process that follows.

Once the budget resolution is in hand, Congress will spend the rest of the year consumed with passing the thirteen appropriations bills, which outline the discretionary spending allocations for each agency during the next fiscal year. Discretionary spending (i.e., Coast Guard budgets, allocations for personnel and programs at the Federal Bureau of Investigation, federal transportation investments), which is about one-third of the federal spending each year, must be distinguished from mandatory spending, which is authorized by permanent laws (so-called "entitlement programs" such as Social Security, Medicare and veterans' benefits). Congress and the president must act each year to provide spending for discretionary programs. While Congress may, they do not have to act on mandatory programs.

Numerous committees and subcommittees are involved in examining the President's Budget and coming up with proposals to reallocate investments and restrict or expand the federal purse. What is important to remember is that the budget process is largely a zero-sum game. This means that failing the allocation of "new money," programs within the budget are balanced off against one another so that one program's gain is another's loss. Appropriations committees differ in terms of flexibility, depending on the "ceiling," i.e., the total amount of money, they have at their disposal. This zero-sum game holds true for the Appropriations Committee as a whole and for the thirteen individual appropriations subcommittees. The zero-sum tradeoff is exacerbated by the hard-and-fast ceiling of the budget cap for all discretionary programs. For example, a desire for an additional billion dollars for the Department of Health and Human Services not included in the President's Budget is tough to translate into reality, because this billion dollars must be extracted from the other appropriations bills. This will require the consent of the other appropriations subcommittees to less money for allocations to the agencies under their jurisdiction. As another example, making room in a $400 billion defense appropriations bill for a new $50 million program is a much easier task than making room for the same level of resources in an $18 billion Foreign Operations appropriations bill. If you are trying to get increased resources for a program within the US foreign affairs budget (the so-called 150 account), it is critical to understand the different pressures—from the White House, the party leadership, the chairman and members of the committee—under which the appropriations subcommittee staff operates. Knowing the boundaries for possible action will ensure that you have realistic expectations and a convincing rationale for your program.

The federal government's fiscal year (FY) stretches from October 1st to September 30th. Officially, the congressional calendar runs from January 20th to early October. However, only very rarely does Congress manage to finish the budget prior to the end of the fiscal year. In order to avoid a federal shutdown, Congress will pass a "continuing resolution" for those appropriations bills not completed; the continuing resolution will allow agencies to operate at current year allocations until a new budget is finalized.

Whereas these days the defense bills are usually the first passed (due to the political pressure and perceptions surrounding the importance of the Pentagon budget to our security and the political demand to "support the troops"), the same does not hold true for either the Commerce-Justice-State appropriations bill, which contains State Department funding, or for the international operations budgets. Late in calendar year 2001 and early 2002, the Defense Department had already received its allocation for fiscal year 2002 programs, because Congress had made passage of the Defense and Military Construction appropriations bills a priority; however, the State Department and USAID allocations for the next year had not yet been acted upon. Despite the substantial increase in activities related to post-conflict Afghanistan, US diplomatic and development agencies had to shift funding from other program areas to fund the burgeoning activities in Afghanistan because their allocation remained at FY2001 levels of funding, a year during which the US had no presence in the country.

The shifting of funds amongst accounts is not exclusively an exercise of non-defense related federal agencies; in fact, this activity has been a common occurrence for the Pentagon in the past dozen years. The Department of Defense often has to move resources out of its operations and maintenance (O&M) and readiness accounts to fund unforeseen operations, a recurring issue in a world where deployments are often for nontraditional missions.

Omnibus Bills

Congress almost always runs out of time to pass the thirteen appropriations bills as separate pieces of legislation. Inevitably, all the appropriations bills that were either not made a priority or whose final ceiling is still a matter of negotiation between the White House and Congress will get rolled together in what is called an "omnibus" appropriations bill. Not only do all of the leftover appropriations bills get wrapped up into a gargantuan piece of legislation, but all "must pass" reauthorizations or fixes to existing statutes usually get tacked onto the omnibus as well. For example, the reauthorization of the State Department often ended up in the omnibus bills passed between 1994 and 2002 because it was not prioritized for actual debate by the full chamber (to use Hill jargon, it was not given floor time). The process of passing an omnibus is extremely murky even to many people working inside Congress.

Emergency Appropriations

An exception to the general rules of budgeting procedure with respect to appropriations legislation is the "emergency supplemental." An emergency supplemental is a request sent from the president to Congress for additional appropriations to cover an unforeseen contingency, thus the "emergency" designation. Unlike the normal budgeting process, emergency requests fall outside of the guidelines set by the Congressional Budget Resolution, as well as the budget caps placed on individual spending bills by the Appropriations Committee. Whereas the normal budgeting process is a zero-sum game—any additional funding for a specific program must be "offset" by a reduction to a different program—emergency supplementals can be increased without "counting" against other programs or objectives.

For example, President Bill Clinton's 1999 emergency supplemental request for military operations in Kosovo came to the Hill at $14 billion; the Republican majority saw an opportunity to "backfill" Pentagon accounts believed to have been shortchanged and passed a $19 billion supplemental. President George W. Bush's 2003 request for $87 billion to continue operations in Iraq and Afghanistan was passed, but not without considerable debate over the $22 billion that was designated for reconstruction as opposed to military operations. By utilizing the option of an emergency supplemental, the difficult zero-sum tradeoff against other desired spending is avoided. Emergency supplementals are a way to "have your cake and eat it too." The reality is that all presidents use the supplemental option in cases of real emergencies as well as for politically expedient purposes.

These are just cursory explanations of the legislative and budget processes and the two major anomalies to regular procedure that are essential to understanding how Congress functions.

AGENCIES AND ACTIVISM

Each of the military departments has a liaison office in both the House and Senate, a program that dates back to the 1960s. Liaisons are at the beck and call of staffers to answer any questions that arise, host lunch briefings on a new weapons system, and generally provide the user-friendly interface between staffers and the Pentagon. They offer numerous trips to view military hardware on-site, and the services often bring their equipment up to Capitol Hill itself with daylong demonstrations in the foyer of a House or Senate office building.

No other agencies had this proximity to, and reach, on Capitol Hill until early 2002, when the State Department established liaison offices on the Hill. It remains to be seen whether these offices will become as effective in working with staff to help increase support for the activities and entities that fall under the State Department's auspices.

Regardless of the location of their offices—whether on the Hill, at the Pentagon, or near Foggy Bottom—all federal employees fall under the same restrictions regarding support of the President's Budget. In short, all federal personnel are required to support the president's annual budget submission. This has not precluded the military services from circulating their "unfunded priorities (or requirements) list" (UPL or UFR), which details the items each service wants that did not make it into the President's Budget. We know of no other agency with a similar standardized process for conveying explicit listings of requirements not funded in the President's Budget to Capitol Hill.

Supporting the President's Budget does not exclude conveying one's honest perspective, however. For example, an Air Force liaison officer might say, "yes, I support the president's request for F-22 acquisition in this year's budget…it's just too bad that the setting of priorities has edged out the procurement dollars needed for Air Force tankers." Or, the State Department liaison could say, "I believe the president was correct to prioritize funding for the Millennium Challenge Account as well as the HIV/AIDS initiative. Unfortunately, the budget pie is too small to allow similar increases to our diplomatic and development efforts in states where Islamic extremism is a powerful force."

GETTING THE MEMBER INVOLVED

Sometimes the most direct and effective way to get a Member's attention on an issue is to actively involve him in a meeting, either in Washington or back in his district/state. Three common ways to meet your legislator are at public meetings he convenes, at an office visit at your request, or at your organization's meetings to which you have invited him. All of these options provide a good opportunity to raise issues of interest to you. (A general rule of thumb on "big picture" and long-term issues is, the earlier in the year the better.) Members will pay more attention to your views if they are presented at a time when their attention is not being pulled in numerous directions. If it is not possible to meet during a recess or work period in the district, then you should check the upcoming floor schedule and committee websites in order to assess whether the Member is swamped with obligations like mark-ups or conference committees. In other words, if your objective is to meet with a member of the Armed Services Committee, don't try to organize it during the mark-up or floor consideration of the defense bill.

Public Meetings

Most Members of Congress have some sort of public forum in their districts where they meet with constituents and answer questions. The number of meetings usually increases around election time. Members of Congress use these meetings to figure out what the main concerns of the community are. These gatherings offer a great opportunity for you to ask specific questions on international cooperative security issues. Even better, if a group of people attend with a couple of different foreign policy questions, the Member will likely leave the meeting thinking that international issues are a significant concern of his constituents. For example, when Members traveled back to their districts during the recess in August 2003, they became intensely aware of constituents' concerns about Iraq; these stories hit the local, as well as the national headlines. Members immediately turned to the Pentagon with the questions raised by their constituents. Whereas there had been almost deafening silence regarding the status and progress in Iraq from the Pentagon earlier in the summer, by the time staff arrived back at their desk in early September, the Pentagon was delivering daily emails on progress in Iraq to all defense staffers.

If you should get an opportunity to meet the Member in a public forum, ask well thought-out, targeted questions that require concrete responses and—if the media is present—questions that can spur positive media coverage. These kinds of questions will portray the Member in a favorable light if he answers the way you would like. In addition, the questions should bring out detailed responses that you can remind your elected leader of later, if necessary.

Following the meeting, write the Member an email or fax. If you agreed with his position on international aid for poverty reduction, express your appreciation and offer your support. If you disagreed with his position, write asking for clarification on the position and state your opinion. If international concerns did not get raised, write a letter asking the questions you had planned to ask.

Office Visits in Washington or in the Home District

A face-to-face meeting with an elected official is sometimes the most effective way to share information, educate, or present your positions on an issue. This is true whether you are going alone or in a coalition with others. It is especially impressive to ask others to join you and go as a group of local experts, opinion leaders for the community, and others whose judgment the Member is likely to respect. Once you have had such a meeting, future letters and other communications may receive closer attention from the Member and his legislative staff. If you choose to go with a group, pay special attention to the tips offered below.

Arranging the Appointment

Schedule a meeting in Washington or in the Member's local office (whichever is most convenient for the Member). The local office can provide a schedule of "district work periods" or other times when the Member is expected to be home. Arrange appointments through the "scheduler." As noted for interactions with staff, be particularly courteous to the Member's scheduler; she determines the legislator's itinerary and performs a "gatekeeper" function in the office. Explain the purpose of the meeting and who will attend. Unless you have an unusual problem, do not ask for more than ten or fifteen minutes. If you are unable to schedule a meeting on your first try, do not give up. You may want to try getting others with existing contacts involved to help schedule a meeting.

Preparing for the Meeting

The importance of preparation cannot be overstated. As mentioned in Chapter 4, once you get access to a Member or staffer, then it is incumbent upon you to fashion your pitch for maximum relevance and impact to elicit future opportunities for dialogue and/or outreach. Keep the following tips in mind:

- Know the Member's record on the specific issues that you want to address.

- Decide on your goal and message.

- Do not try to debate the issue with the Member. You are there to deliver a message or ask prepared questions, i.e., "Would you be our keynote speaker on Congress and security issues post-September 11th?" Make it highly focused.

- Have facts and figures ready, but do not overwhelm your audience with these. Be ready to answer questions and to respond to counterarguments made by your opponents.

- Be prepared to leave behind information that the Member's staff can use, including fact sheets on your organization and on the issue you are concerned about. Include one or two of your favorite websites for references, and remember that brevity is key.

When a meeting involves a coalition of other organizations or individuals, remember the following, in addition to the above:

- Send your most effective spokespersons.

- Be sure all participants know the Member's record on your issues.

- Agree on your goal and message beforehand. Show a united front; divisiveness is irritating and confusing.

- Have a single spokesperson who can call on others to add information when necessary.

A Successful Meeting

Even though you scheduled an appointment with your Member, you may find that he has been called away and that you are meeting with a staffer. Do not dismay! These aides have a great deal of influence with Members of Congress. And it is important that they understand your issues, too. Whether meeting with Members or staffers, keep the following in mind:

- Be respectful. Even if you consistently disagree with your Member, approach your differences in a courteous, constructive manner.

- Make your presentation simple and straightforward.

- Avoid small talk. Members of Congress and their staffs are used to people asking for things. The sooner you make clear your intent, the better they will be able to help.

- Establish common ground. Thank the Member for a recent vote, sponsorship of a bill, or for public statements on an important issue.

- Do not use a lot of statistics. They will not be remembered. Do use a few directly relevant, memorable numbers to illustrate your point.

- Avoid jargon and acronyms.

- Be a good listener. Remember, the educational process is a two-way street. Let the Member ask questions as you go along, and answer with hard facts and clear examples.

- If you do not know the answer to a question, do not fake it. Say, "I don't know, but I will get back to you on it." Then do it.

- Do not assume the Member is against your position just because he asks hostile-sounding questions. He may simply be finding out how to answer the arguments of opponents of your view.

- Get a commitment. Will the Member support you, oppose you, or at least keep an open mind?

- Do not linger. Thank your Member and/or staff for their time and leave politely.

- Follow up on the meeting. Send a thank you note. Invite the legislator to an upcoming event.

Invitations to Visit your Organization or Speak at Events

Invite your Member to speak at a luncheon, dinner, or special event. An accepted invitation forces the Member to study your concerns and it initiates a relationship. You can suggest a topic relevant to your group's interests. A staffer will be assigned to research the topic, and often the staffer will learn about new areas that may be of interest to the Member. If the Member ignores you repeatedly, then build an even wider supportive coalition on the issue and try again later.

Questions asked following the presentation can also influence the Member. Quite often the question and answer period will teach the Member more than he originally knew about the topic. If asked about legislation with which he is unfamiliar, a Member will usually respond that he will look into it. That alone is a good thing.

Remember that Members and their staffs are not omniscient. Hundreds of bills get introduced in each session of a Congress. Simply bringing a piece of legislation to their attention is often helpful.

Organizing an Event Outside of Washington

A supportive and visible local constituency for peace and security issues is the single most important factor behind strong representation of these issues in the US Congress. Members of Congress usually spend most of their district time attending to local concerns and domestic issues. A chance to engage with constituents on international issues is refreshing and rare. Local events can be anything from a press conference or speech to an issue forum or debate. Members may also organize hearings or town-hall meetings in the district or attend conferences, especially if given the opportunity for a featured speaking or moderating role. These events are a powerful way for Members to convey their ideas and their image to the public.

There are several ways to connect with your elected leaders on peace and security issues. The most common ways are individual meetings and group events with a focus on an international topic or policy. With respect to group events, keep in mind that:

- Events should be organized by people who live in the district or state and who therefore vote in elections.

- Elected leaders like to participate in events that make them look good. A savvy Member will understand that events are vehicles to assist in accomplishing broader legislative initiatives and political goals; they should not be ends in themselves. A savvy organizer will consult with the local office in the planning stages of an event to make sure the Member's needs are met to the fullest extent possible.

- An event will be much more meaningful and attractive to the Member if it is tied to a familiar platform, or to an issue on which he has some background knowledge.

- Elected leaders assiduously avoid events where the audience can play "gotcha"—i.e., corner him, and either monopolize his time or berate him.

Also, be aware of ethics rules for Members of Congress with regards to local events, i.e., where it is held and what types of activities may take place. Public venues and educational facilities—such as libraries and universities—are usually safe bets.

Planning Pays Off

Some of the preparation tips for planning a district event are similar to preparing for an individual meeting. Being familiar with the Member's issues, interests, and responsibilities is as important as being clear about what you would like the Member to do for you. However, a local event is different in that you and your organization will extend an invitation to the Member to participate in an activity over which he and his staff will have limited control. Local events are a good way to build his appreciation for your organization's issues, as well as his confidence in your support on those issues. Your credibility as an individual or organization is on the line with such events, so it is vital to thoroughly prepare when finding a venue, setting the agenda, and determining who will be invited to attend.

Scour the Member's website so that you know his interests, particularly any international peace and security angles. Make sure to check the "press" or "breaking news" section of the website to see if he has participated recently in any local events on international topics or issued press releases about peace and security. If so, you might be able to collaborate with a local entity that has already convened a successful event. Call the sponsoring organization or individual! Explain your interest and ask if you could speak with the person who organized the event. Developing a supportive political constituency for peace and security issues will ultimately require such collaboration and mutual support.

Even though most Members do not actually serve on the International Relations or Armed Services Committees, a Member will often speak on the floor or give speeches about his peace and security concerns. Check the website for speeches or floor statements about international issues. Also, during recess, many Members of the House and Senate travel abroad. You might find a way to integrate a news item into your own event. For example, if the Member has recently traveled abroad—say, visited US troops on a trip to Africa—you might want to structure your event so he can report on the trip, share impressions, and then answer some questions about related issues. Be sensitive to the fact that Members often receive bad press for foreign travel. Make sure the Member welcomes such an opportunity first.

Check your local paper's archives to see if your Member has participated in prior events about peace and security. Was the coverage favorable? Was it a productive session? Was there a picket line? What about hecklers in the audience? This is important information because often, if a Member has had a negative experience with such events, he will be reluctant to participate in another one unless it is shown to be significantly different.

Sign up for the Member's "email newsletter" so you can receive regular notification of upcoming public events. Attend a couple of events, if possible. This will give you an idea of the types of events in which he participates. It will also give you a first-hand view of how an event is organized. Make mental notes of how an event could be improved or how you would frame an issue for such a venue. Sign up for a few state and national organizations' e-newsletters, as they often contain information about events framed in a politically savvy way. (There are many options available. Start with the Foreign Policy Association at www.fpa.org, which has a resource library with a search engine.)

As we have noted, international issues are not always a priority for Members of Congress. Senators tend to have more reasons to become involved in international issues than their counterparts in the House. If you do not find any good angles or entry points for peace and security issues, do not despair. Your event may help initiate a new issue area for the Member. In this case, it will be necessary to structure your event as an all-around education opportunity for the Member. Here are some sample events to which you might consider inviting a Member of Congress.

- Suppose you are interested in peacekeeping. Organize an event at a local school or university and invite a person with recent peacekeeping experience to come and engage in a dialogue with a local academic expert or international affairs professional. Structure and facilitate the discussion so that the peacekeeper recounts "on the ground" stories and the academic provides the "big picture" commentary relating the stories to the US in the world. You could spur another interesting discussion by inviting an older veteran to come and speak with a recently returned peacekeeper. Ask them to compare experiences. Ask the Member of Congress to comment on their presentations, but do not require it. Sometimes Members are happy to provide brief remarks and then sit and learn with the rest of the audience.

- Suppose you are interested in homeland security. Organize an event at a local venue that features firefighters and medical personnel who have benefited from education and training about crisis prevention and response. Inquire at your local fire station, hospital, or with public health officials as to whether anyone recently attended national or international conferences. Invite the attendees to be the featured speakers.

- Suppose you are interested in international exchange programs. Organize an event at the local high school with exchange students and the Member of Congress. Structure the discussion so that the main theme is how international exchanges promote mutual understanding, can help counter extremist ideology, and highlight international conflict resolution. Make sure to highlight specific cases in which international exchange alumni have helped promote American values and bolstered its image abroad. Make sure to give the federal government credit for supporting such programs.

- Suppose you are interested in nuclear threat reduction and nonproliferation. Examine the potential local implications of commitments made in the 2002 Moscow Treaty. If there are nuclear weapons laboratories or facilities in your district or state, organize an event surrounding the potential implications of this Treaty to their activities. If no facilities are located in your area, organize an event with local businesses that have been working with Russian weapons scientists to create commercial opportunities for their technological innovations.[1]

If your Member of Congress has limited exposure to peace and security issues in the district, working with a local educator is a good way to start. The Member of Congress can be invited to come engage in a dialogue with a class. This is an easy option because the venue and the audience are ready-made and it is a "feel-good" setting.

The Event Itself

Give yourself a lot of time to organize an event with a Member of Congress. Generally, it is more difficult to get a time slot on a senator's calendar than a representative's, because senators must pay attention to the needs of far more constituents. Meet with a local office staffer. Ask about her experience in local event participation. What does she suggest? What was the best event the Member ever attended and why? Does she have a list of like-minded organizations that she could share with you? Ask about events that the Member himself cosponsored or collaborated on. Is that a possibility for your event? Remember, however, if a

---

[1] For information about US businesses involved in US-Russia nonproliferation efforts, go to the United States Industry Coalition website at: www.usic.net.

Member directly collaborates on the event, his office will want some control over the agenda, including the title, guests, and content. If you do cosponsor an activity involving a Member, make sure that the message is coordinated and that you are in frequent communication with his staff.

A Cautionary Tale

Here is a short vignette that illustrates what can go wrong with a Member-sponsored event. Keep in mind that, in the end, everything worked out, but not without a few tense moments. (Details have been changed to preserve anonymity.)

In 2002, a friend helped organize a town hall meeting for her Member of Congress, who represented an East Coast district famous for its liberal activism. It was her hope to engage a broad public conversation about US peace and security interests after September 11th. She wanted the discussion to be about the recent US intervention in Afghanistan and the prospects for long-term stability in the region. She also wanted to "bring the issue home" to the district. In order to do this, she had secured the participation of the last US Chief Political Officer to Afghanistan (who also happened to be a constituent). The second speaker was a local retired Army helicopter pilot who had been deployed twice to Somalia, once with the Army and once with the UN. These two speakers had broad experience and understanding, and said they felt comfortable addressing a large public audience. She provided the two speakers with a framework of themes for the event, plus five specific questions for them to answer. The plan was for the Member of Congress to introduce the session and the speakers, and then hand the program over to a professional facilitator. (This was the Member's self-selected role at the forum.)

Our friend secured an agreement from a well-respected statewide international affairs organization to help publicize the event on its website and notify its membership. She also researched and found several local newsletters online that published notices for upcoming community events. She made sure to notify local schools, retirement homes, veterans' organizations, and military clubs affiliated with the National Guard and Reserves.

All the plans went along smoothly until she realized that she had not completely controlled the publicity message about the event. Without a thorough discussion, the Member's local office had added another region of the world to the title of the event. The title advertised on the official press release stated: "US Security and Conflict Resolution: Afghanistan and the Middle East." They did this because so many people in the district were interested in the Israeli-Palestinian conflict, and had been clamoring lately for more action from the Member. At this point, there was nothing our friend could do to retract the press release, so she hoped for the best, informed the speakers that the Israeli-Palestinian issue might come up, and went ahead preparing for the event.

The night of the event came, and upon her arrival at the university she was greeted by a large group of people picketing and holding up signs protesting US policy in the Middle East. They were looking forward to an opportunity to put the Member of Congress on the spot and on the record regarding her position on their issue. Luckily, our friend had organized the agenda so that the Member would not be on the dais during the question and answer session, so direct confrontations were avoided. The savvy Member also made sure to address the demonstrators' concerns in her opening remarks, which did much to alleviate the tension. Finally, our friend went outside and extended an invitation to the entire group of demonstrators to join the audience, which some of them then did.

So what is the main lesson? That you and your Member of Congress may well have different objectives for an event on peace and security. Make sure this is discussed and accommodated to the extent possible, but do everything you can to prevent surprises, including having only one title and event description.

ADDITIONAL TIPS

After you have researched the Member and decided on a theme, survey the local landscape of organizations. Which ones have an interest in peace and security issues? Civic organizations, churches, veterans, students, and retirees are often candidates for collaboration. What about peace and security groups from the past? Is there a peace studies, conflict resolution, or a ROTC program at the local college? Does your town have a sister-city program? Try to think creatively. Remember, since September 11th, peace and security issues have become much more significant to our nation, as well as to many citizens who previously had no direct personal or professional contact with the issues.

Decide whether or not you would like others to collaborate with you to organize the event. Having more than one organization involved can help divide the preparatory tasks, but it also might dilute the focus of the gathering. It also makes controlling the message more of a challenge. The agenda details must be worked out explicitly before any announcement or public notice of the event itself. (Some organizations might not require that they be consulted on the agenda, but would be willing to help publicize or issue invitations. Ask them.)

Decide whether or not this event will be open to the public. If yes, then you must find an accessible venue with parking. What do you want to call it? Remember, "town hall meeting" has certain connotations, such as an open microphone and a free-ranging question-and-answer period. Will there be an open microphone? Will you accept written questions on note cards? Will you have a facilitator? What type of literature will be made available, and from which organizations? Will you control what other people bring to distribute? Open meetings attract all kinds of participants. Sometimes you need someone prepared to be a gentle bouncer. Find out about the security arrangements at the venue.

Make sure you have a solid audience commitment if you plan to advertise this event to the Member as a large group activity. (Remember, elected leaders see voters in every audience.) Don't overreach. A well-organized small group event is always preferable to a helter-skelter large group event. Also, keep in mind that a good-sized audience in a too-tight venue makes a better impression than the same number of people in a cavernous facility.

Finally, it is not a bad idea to find a basic event-planning guide or checklist. After all, even when the subject of discussion is international peace and security, the key to a successful event is always the simple nuts-and-bolts of good organizing.

ON-THE-HILL OUTREACH

Planning an event on Capitol Hill would follow the same basic guidelines above, though a Hill event involving Members (as opposed to staff) will likely be more media-intense and thus carry higher stakes. Special events that include Members but that are *not* designed to capture media attention tend to cater either to an influential political action committee or a high-powered local delegation visiting DC. The following outlines some of the most essential ingredients for events or outreach on Capitol Hill.

Events on the Hill

The most essential ingredient for launching any event on Capitol Hill is a knowledgeable and willing staffer to assist with content, timing, and outreach. No substitute exists for insider assistance, not only because rooms on the Hill are only available to Members, but also because an insider can help you wade through the peculiarities of the political atmosphere and the possible challenges of timing for the event. Remember to help the staffer help you. For example, if the office has agreed to be the official sponsor, you can write the draft of the "Dear Colleague" letter that will be circulated to announce the event. It is also important to ensure that the staffer has all the information she needs (room set-up, audio-visual equipment, etc.) so that she can assist you in the least time-consuming manner possible.

Informational events on the Hill are generally more useful for staff than for Members. One-on-one meetings with Members are more effective and a better way to get their attention. By including Members in informational events, you raise the stakes of the dialogue, as well as the formalities related to who gets credit and who gets recognized first. In addition, Members are driven by media attention, so getting their participation may completely undermine the "educational" objectives of the endeavor. Lastly, organizing an event for Members may be an exercise in "herding cats" and may completely fall flat due to unforeseen events. If the Member (or Members) who has (have) agreed to sponsor your event would like to be involved, then the best role for him would most likely be to kick off the event. (He will most likely have to leave immediately thereafter for a floor vote, a hearing, or a press conference, etc.)

The Logistics

There are several initial tasks that must be addressed in order to run an event on the Hill. First, only Member's offices can reserve rooms on the Hill, so the most immediate need is having a Member's office that will at least reserve you a room, if not sponsor your event. Ideally, you have a Hill office's support to work "in collaboration" or "in partnership" with you to pull all the pieces together for the event. (Note: Members cannot "cosponsor" an event on the Hill for you unless the event deals only with US federal agencies as collaborators. The word "cosponsor" may connote undue influence or the exchange of funds or resources.) Assistance from a Member's office in getting a room is not the same thing as sponsorship. If a Member agrees to sponsor an event, that means it is an event officially sanctioned by and emanated from his office. The trade-off involved in this option is that his office staff becomes the primary organizer and agenda-setter of the event. This option requires more insider tasks as well, such as getting signatures and clearing the topic with all offices involved. This gets more complicated as more Members are added, and potentially even more complicated in an attempt to garner bipartisan support.

So, if the Member jumps on board eagerly, it means you'll have less control. You may still be a valued advisor, but it will be different than your organization serving as the headliner and the recognized sponsor. You can gauge whether or not to "hand off" your event to the office after your office visit. What is the level of interest or seeming commitment? Does the staffer understand the substance and appear facile with the political terrain? Generally, a Member sponsored event is most desirable because of the increased possibilities for getting the word out to staff. Also, bipartisan support is a critical element to maximize your outreach capacity. Details of room reservations are laid out later in this chapter.

Content and Framing

First and foremost, all of the discussions in the previous chapter about framing, terminology, clear and concise findings, and recommendations should apply to the content of any event in Congress. In fact, as you will be addressing a larger audience than one staffer or Member, it will be critical to be well-versed in the political landscape surrounding your issue and what aspects of the topic to either avoid or address indirectly, so as to mitigate potential negative feedback.

In Chapter 4, we briefly covered "third rail" issues, where even discussions of the facts are distorted by strong political or emotional extremes. One way to engage the issues while keeping the discussion in problem-solving mode is to address it indirectly and offer pragmatic, politically feasible next steps.

For example, the role of the Comprehensive Test Ban Treaty in furthering US nonproliferation objectives and other security interests is highly contentious. Scientists and policy experts alike dispute the ability to verify potential cheating under the CTBT; many of those same people also argue that the "safety, reliability, and performance" of the US nuclear deterrent cannot be maintained indefinitely without testing. Others, however, argue that US ratification of the CTBT is the lynchpin for sustaining the Nuclear Nonproliferation Treaty as well as attaining other US nonproliferation objectives. All of these arguments and more came to the fore in the debate on the Comprehensive Test Ban Treaty prior to its defeat in the Senate in 1999. At this writing, the Administration supports a continued US moratorium on testing, but it is adamantly opposed to this treaty. For now, the CTBT is a "third rail" issue.

If you are addressing congressional staffers on your recommendations for strengthening the Nuclear Nonproliferation Treaty, it would be fine to discuss in detail the disarmament commitments of the recognized nuclear states, but any mention of the CTBT would have to be treated very delicately. You might, for example, say: "A commitment to a zero-yield ban on nuclear testing could play a positive role in preventing erosion of the treaty; however, legitimate concerns exist regarding the maintenance of the US arsenal without testing, as well as questions related to verification of the ban. Perhaps a critical first step would be to initiate confidence-building measures with key actors of concern in order to more fully instill confidence in US verification capabilities."

Notice that CTBT was not referenced explicitly. Also note that both the advantages of a test ban and the basic questions raised by those against it were referenced. Further, note the positive and politically feasible recommendations for overcoming questions about verification. Lastly, the proposed confidence-building measures to bolster US confidence in its ability to detect nuclear tests would be advantageous, whether or not the CTBT ever goes into effect.

Speakers and Format

Once you have willing Hill offices in place, you must decide on the format, timing, and other details related to packaging your presentation and maximizing your outreach. Our recipe for success with our *Security for a New Century* briefings, which will be covered in more detail in the next chapter, is based on the following guidelines:

- The briefings formally last only one hour. This allows busy staff to make the commitment and know they can leave at the hour. Staff simply cannot partake in anything that would extend beyond an hour and a half. An hour alone is a big commitment on any one topic in light of all the other issues they have to juggle.

- A maximum of two speakers are chosen in light of the time constraints. We have found that pairing an academic or policy analyst with their operational counterpart can make for a very effective duo, bridging the gap between theory and practice. The academic can offer the big picture of how global change has impacted the subject at hand and put the topic into context. Operational experts offer a "ground truth" perspective that most Hill audiences will find not only interesting, but also quite persuasive.

- The speakers are given twenty minutes in total, with the remaining forty minutes dedicated to discussion. After being offered the basics—why the topic is relevant to US security, why Congress should care, and what Congress can do about it—staff can follow up with their specific questions related to the subject. As mentioned, staff will have a wide range of backgrounds and levels of knowledge. Talking at them for an hour may not provide anything relevant to their specific tasks; a discussion with them will lend itself to problem-solving, ensure that their questions get addressed, and have a greater impact. Remember, the educational process is a two-way street.

- The timing of the briefing is absolutely critical. Monday afternoons and Friday mornings are ideal for staff briefings, because most Members are still back in the district and staff may have time to escape for an hour. In the House, Tuesday mornings are sometimes good if they don't convene until late that day; the same goes for Thursday afternoons, if they recess early. In both the House and Senate, if the event must take place between Tuesday and Thursday, meeting during the lunch hour works best.

- Minimize the formalities and maximize the substance. Remember, the Hill is a fast-paced, competitive environment. If staffers take time to show up, they already believe the speakers have something of value to impart. Don't waste their time with a lengthy reading of the speakers' qualifications. Get to the point.

- Do not include media, and make the discussion "off-the-record." This will lower the stakes substantially and help create an environment that encourages open and honest dialogue. Including media will likely ensure that staffers use questions to score political points, rather than learn more about the subject. Media presence denotes a distinct type of event. On the Hill, dialogue is not served well by media presence as it changes the dynamic in the room. In contrast, an off-the-Hill event may be organized purposefully to include a photo-op.

- If the presentation includes Power Point slides or overheads, these might be offered as a handout at the event. Or, a user-friendly fact sheet—two pages maximum—covering the main points can be a useful tool.

Outreach for the event will probably entail invitations sent by you with follow-up phone calls to targeted committees or Member offices. Many groups in DC have electronic notification lists of staffers for foreign policy and defense. Further, Member offices often have their own lists tailored to their specific legislative objectives. You may want to explore whether you can collaborate with another DC-based group to use their list information or explore with your sponsoring offices what lists they might be able to access to help maximize outreach. A portion of the outreach will almost always entail the use of a "Dear Colleague" letter. Obviously, this will be a decision that must be left to the Member offices that are lending their support.

"Dear Colleague" Letters

A "Dear Colleague" letter is an official correspondence that is distributed in bulk to Members, committees, and other offices. The letter is written on official letterhead, contains official business, and must be signed by a Member of Congress. They are a good way for Members to notify each other about important issues, request co-sponsorship of legislation, remind staff and Members of upcoming events, or circulate a good op-ed piece.

In the House, this letter requires an accompanying cover letter, signed by a representative with specific distribution instructions as to which committees and which representatives will receive the letter. For a Senate "Dear Colleague," someone from a senator's office must take the final letter to a services department and fill out a distribution form answering questions similar to the ones above.

Please note that a "Dear Colleague" cannot be used to notify members of an event taking place on the Hill that is sponsored by an outside organization, with the exception of federally-funded agencies. However, after initial invitations have been sent to Members (and/or staff) by the outside organization, a "Dear Colleague" can be used to remind others on the Hill about the event.

OTHER RESOURCES, TIPS, AND TOOLS

Researching a Member

If a Member is not an internationalist before he gets to the Hill, he probably will not be one after he is elected, unless his committee assignment forces it upon him. Just like your circle of friends and family, individuals are already internationally-minded based on a life experience or interest—or they are not. This is not a good or bad judgment, it just means that non-internationally minded Members have a steeper learning curve and that any strategy to capture their interest might require more domestic "hooks" or a long-term outreach plan. This is where it is important to know a Member's background. Were his parents immigrants? Did he live abroad? Did she serve in the military? Belong to the Rotary Club? Host exchange students? What was his undergraduate major?

The task of researching Members and their interests in international cooperation or security has been made dramatically easier with the advent of the Internet. For purposes of researching Members and legislative initiatives, the websites of the following institutions are indispensable:

- The House of Representatives (www.house.gov). This includes links to each Member's website, all committees, oversight plans, press releases, and up-to-the-minute legislative action.

- The Senate (www.senate.gov). This contains the same useful content as the House.

- The Library of Congress (www.loc.gov). The Library of Congress is the institutional memory of the United States Congress; it is a research resource and a treasure trove of information. Of particular importance for citizen outreach is the legislative research engine THOMAS (http://thomas.loc.gov).

A Member's individual website will often include much biographical information, and highlight issues of importance to the district. It will list the committee responsibilities of the Member and list the Member's membership in organizations internal to the Congress itself, such as a particular task force, study group, or caucus. Sometimes interesting non-curricular activities like district events or speaking engagements show up in the press section, so make sure to check that as well.

At first glance, it may seem that your Member does not sit on any committees with jurisdiction over cooperative security issues. But make sure you dig deeper to see if he is on the Nonproliferation Task Force or the Army Caucus. Sometimes just being asked by enough constituents will prompt a Member to join such a caucus or task force. If there is a large ethnic minority in your district, your Member might even belong to an ethnic heritage-based group like the India Caucus. For instance, if your Member is not particularly international, but is on the India Caucus, there are numerous cross-cutting issues you could raise: nuclear nonproliferation, regional stability in South Asia, resource scarcity and population growth, economic development, Indian contributions to UN peacekeeping, and so forth.

THOMAS will allow you to search for legislation in the current or past sessions of Congress. You can also search the full texts of bills, either by bill number or by word/phrase. In addition, you can search by subject term, status in the legislative process, date of introduction or floor action, sponsor/cosponsor, or committee of jurisdiction. Finally, you can also search the *Congressional Record* for items of interest.

If you are planning to visit your own elected representatives, search the Member's name together with a phrase like "international cooperation" or "human rights" in order to find out if he is on the record with regard to your topic of interest. Have a few key search phrases and words in mind. Also try your search with different countries and with organizations like the UN or NATO.

If you do find a piece of legislation relevant to your interests, you can gather even more information. Who introduced the bill(s)? Is it bipartisan? How many cosponsors are signed on? Is the bill moving through the legislative process? When was the last time any action was taken? Who has spoken on the issue already? As we mentioned earlier, take note of the "unusual suspects" as you conduct research.

The documentation available online is a good place to start, but a truly sophisticated strategy must include some insights into what makes a Member "tick." Who does the Member listen to, what personal experiences may figure into his perspectives, and how do certain issues play in his district? If you can build a solid knowledge base about the Member's particular passions and political interests, then you can try working the local political pulse in a more favorable direction. Are agricultural or manufacturing issues a big local concern? Can you tie your issue to either of those and then join other groups tied to those local concerns to garner access to the Member or build a broad-based constituency?

Congressional Research Service Reports

The CRS is an entire staff of individuals who work in the Library of Congress as issue specialists, serving the Members of both the House and the Senate. They provide Congress with research, analysis, and information on public policy and legislative and legal issues. CRS reserves its direct resources and products exclusively for Congress. That said, some of these reports can be located on websites accessible by the general public.

The way you, as a constituent, may enjoy the use of topical reports by CRS is by making a formal request to your own Member's office. The staffer you talk to can usually do a quick check online and let you know what reports are the most recent and which are available; she can also send you documents electronically or by US mail. This research engine is not available outside of Member offices, however, so it would be good to have one or two specific requests that the staffer can quickly check for you. (Example: "Could you please check to see if there are any CRS reports available on the International Criminal Court and also on the 2002 Nuclear Posture Review?")

CRS reports are occasionally dense, but because they are written for time-pressed staffers and Members, they are user-friendly. These reports are also important because CRS researchers are the gateway for authoritative information that reaches Congress. They are nonpartisan and substantive; balanced, excellent content is their goal. The reports themselves are a good model of how to present solid, substantive educational information to the Hill.

House/Senate Directories

Find a "hard copy" of a House and Senate directory. This will require a bit of sleuthing. There are many directory resources and expensive subscriptions out there touting ways to "know the Hill." The plain old House and Senate directories are valuable tools with lots of insider information in them that commercial variants overlook. A good way to get such a directory is to simply call your Member's office and ask for an old copy that they are getting ready to throw away. Updated directories are published every six months in the House (about once a year in the Senate). When this happens, each office is given a dozen or so copies. The next day, all the old copies will be in the recycling bin. While it is unlikely that you'll get a new issue, the only slightly dated ones are just as helpful for our purposes. Inside you'll find a wealth of information, including lists of caucuses, the internal administrative offices of Congress, and the committee and subcommittee divisions. You'll also be able to see how many staff are allocated to each committee, as well as how many work for the majority and how many work for the minority. Although much of this information is also available online, these directories put it all in one place.

House and Senate Rules and Regulations

Members of Congress have a wide range of opportunities and venues in which to exercise their interests and influence, but all activities related to their official capacities are restrained by codes of ethics and rules of official conduct. These rules are maintained with the intent of keeping congressional deliberations as free from undue influence and special interests as possible. Like many bureaucratic rules, these codes are complex and sometimes confusing. They also evolve and change, depending on who is in power.

One way to reduce such fears is to know ahead of time what the ethics restrictions are before requesting that the Member participate or help organize an event. Both the House and Senate Ethics Committees publish entire ethics manuals, both of which are available online. Be sure to check out the chapters dealing with Member involvement with official and unofficial organizations for the basic guidelines that may apply.

Get A Room

The House and Senate have different designations for rooms and different procedures for securing them. Yet in both chambers the two most important items in convening a Hill briefing are a room and a helpful staffer. Although it seems very basic, sometimes the most difficult part of convening a Hill briefing is securing a room. As we have said, only Members of Congress and their staffs may reserve rooms on behalf of outside organizations or constituents. Below is some information that will help you be prepared when you are requesting the help of a Hill staffer. Keep in mind that you need to make your proposal "yes-able" from the very first meeting.

Committee rooms

In both the House and Senate, committee rooms are controlled by the majority party's committee chair. Each committee has a staff person in charge of scheduling for the room. Some committees are responsive and helpful to all Members, regardless of party affiliation; some are not. The important thing is to have as many options as possible. Every member of a committee should be able to request a time slot for a staff briefing in either the main hearing room or else in one of the smaller hearing rooms. Committee rooms exist in every House and Senate office building. They come in different sizes and shapes, and also come with different kinds of equipment. Some committee rooms require a faxed request form to confirm the reservations; others do not. It is vital that you ascertain whether this is a requirement and follow up on it.

Be mindful of the regular committee schedule when requesting rooms. Aside from recess periods, February through July and September to October are heavily scheduled months, making committee rooms scarcer (especially on Tuesdays, Wednesdays, and Thursdays). Briefings scheduled in a committee hearing room can also get bumped at the last minute for official committee business.

On a side note, there are plusses and minuses about convening a staff briefing when the Members are in recess. Discuss this issue with your staff contact. Our experience suggests that the success of a recess briefing depends on your target audience and at what point during the recess you hold your briefing.

Special events rooms

Special Events is a coordinating office that schedules and maintains several rooms in the House. The rooms are available on a first-come, first-serve basis. They are spread around in different House office buildings and seat between thirty and 230 people. Reservations require an A-2 form, signed by the Member. These forms are available online to House staff.

A different group of rooms in this category includes the "multi-purpose" rooms. There are twenty-five of these rooms available, but most come with certain restrictions. Some reservations are contingent on food being served (the internal House caterer must be used or else the organizer pays a hefty fee). Therefore, it is important to specify whether or not food will be served when calling for availability.

In the Senate, only a handful of "special events" rooms exist. Scheduling of these rooms goes through the Rules Committee via a faxed request that staff can download from an internal Senate website. The staffer must work with a separate office to arrange setup for the room. Depending on the audio-visual equipment required for a briefing, two or more offices may also apply. For example, an overhead, a projector for digital slides, and a screen must be requested through the Sergeant at Arms' office in the Senate; the equipment for showing a video or DVD is only available through the Senate Recording Studio.

Self-schedule rooms

There are ten self-schedule rooms scattered throughout the House office buildings. These rooms are usually smaller, and can only be reserved one week in advance, beginning at 10:00 a.m. on the preceding Friday. The staffer must use the internal intranet system to reserve the room. These rooms do not require any forms and they are good for more informal events and group discussions.

Architect of the Capitol

The Architect controls one room in the Capitol Building—EF 100—which is a beautiful old room that will hold about fifty people. The Congressional staffer must contact the Architect in order to reserve the room. (Note: this room will be closed until the Capitol Visitor's Center construction is concluded. Also note that the acoustics in this room are not good, and it can be quite chilly in the winter.)

Speaker/Majority Leader rooms

The Speaker of the House controls six rooms. Five are in the Capitol itself. They are the "HC" rooms in a new addition adjacent to the basement of the Capitol. The sixth room is the Cannon Caucus Room, a grand hearing room on the second floor of the Cannon Building. The Speaker's office requires an A-1 reservation form, signed by the Member.

The Majority Leader in the Senate controls three rooms in the Capitol. All three of these are large and ornate. The smallest of the three, the Mansfield Room, is rather austere, but is a nice room for a panel discussion that will be well attended. However, this room is very hard to get, which means it must be reserved far in advance. To reserve any of these rooms, the staffer must fax a letter signed by the Member indicating the date, time, and title of the event, as well as specifics on set-up for the room. The Senate also has a handful of "SC" rooms adjacent to the "HC" rooms. The Rules Committee handles the scheduling of these rooms; these rooms are available to individuals and organizations through their home-state senator.

Post-September 11th Security

Prior to September 11th, visitors could wander in and out of the Capitol at will. Public access to the Capitol is currently largely restricted to staff-guided tours. People wishing to get access not on a tour must present a picture ID and have a specific reason for being there (i.e., a meeting with a senator in his "hideaway" or a media event). The exact rules guiding access to the Capitol frequently change. However, we would recommend that you avoid using a room in the Capitol, especially if many Hill outsiders and nongovernmental employees will be attending.

Other House and Senate buildings remain open to the public, but security is tight. For example, trying to take packages or boxes into the building that are too large for the X-ray machine usually will require a trip to Capitol police headquarters so the contents can be inspected.

Putting the Pieces Together:
The Story of *Security for a New Century*

What foreign policy priority can the oil industry, environmentalists, the Quakers, the Bush White House, Senate Democrats, and the US Navy all agree on? Support for US ratification of the UN Law of the Sea Convention. Originally negotiated in 1982 and substantially modified to accommodate US concerns through negotiations concluded in 1994, the Convention constitutes the legal framework governing the world's oceans. With Senate Foreign Relations Committee approval of this Convention by a unanimous vote of 15-0 in February of 2004 and White House support, quick US ratification appeared certain. However, the majority opinion in favor of this convention is not carrying the day.

At this writing, the status of the Law of the Sea Convention exemplifies several of the problems addressed in previous chapters. A handful of anti-treaty pundits—referring to this Convention as the Law of the Sea Treaty (LOST)—have proceeded to overstate the decision-making authority of the United Nations under the Convention, misconstrue its impact on US intelligence gathering, and falsely assess the impediments it imposes on President Bush's Proliferation Security Initiative.[1] The impact of this small group is reverberating with the White House during an election year as well as the Senate Majority Leader's willingness to prioritize floor time for Senate

---

[1] The Convention provides no decision-making role for the UN; the US military (which is responsible for all intelligence operations of relevance) has stated the convention has no impact on their activities; and the Chairman of the Joint Chiefs of Staff and the Chief of Naval Operations confirm that US ratification would facilitate efforts under the Proliferation Security Initiative. See Senator Richard G. Lugar, "The Law of the Sea Convention: The Case for Senate Action," address at the Brookings Institution, May 4, 2004, available online at http://www.brookings.edu/comm/events/20040504lugar.htm

deliberations and a vote. Despite broad consensus among informed citizens and policymakers, Senate ratification during this session appears unlikely. Waning political will, competing political priorities, the time constraints of the congressional calendar, and a pending presidential election are all interrelated factors delaying action clearly in the US interest. The public feedback imbalance of a vocal, well-organized minority encapsulated in this example pervades the current policymaking process on the Hill and requires a nuts and bolts strategy to overcome.

Thus far, we have laid out the urgent needs that must be met, along with the institutional obstacles that hinder change and reinforce persistent imbalances in the approach to "security" as it is considered in Congress. We have also discussed different examples of security issues as they relate to committee structures and congressional staffers, and offered extensive tips and tools on how to do the spadework prior to engaging the Hill. How might all these concerns, constraints, and connections be translated into an action plan?

This chapter details an education strategy for Congress that was implemented in the late 1990s and continues today. The following description is not meant to illustrate a typical strategy, but rather to offer a case study of how carefully organized research and networking, along with the formation of strategic partnerships, can result in a successful program for dialogue on peace and security issues within the US Congress.

THE STORY OF *SECURITY FOR A NEW CENTURY*

Security for a New Century (*SNC*) is an ongoing briefing series—also known as a "study group"[2]—for Congress. The *SNC* study group meets regularly with US and international policy professionals to discuss the post-Cold War and post-September 11th security environment. *SNC* was founded in 1998 by a staffer and three Members of Congress concerned about the lack of

---

[2] The term "study group" was chosen because it had no existing rules and regulations associated with it, and because it conveyed the general objective of the briefing series: increasing understanding of emerging international security challenges by serving as a cutting-edge educational resource for congressional staff.

substantive and informal gatherings on the Hill to discuss new security challenges. The elimination of the Arms Control and Foreign Policy Caucus in 1995 and the increased partisanship had rendered Congress bereft of such informal bipartisan venues. The acute need for such cooperative, problem-solving opportunities became obvious in the wake of the Cold War, when elected leaders lacked clear consensus on foreign policy priorities. Important government programs that were created to address topics like rule of law and peacekeeping did not garner widespread recognition in Congress. These and other security issues—nuclear threat reduction, democratic transition aid, and even issues of terrorism—were falling between the cracks of the existing committee system and therefore were not receiving the attention that they deserved.

The study group was created with the benefit of initial research and insights garnered during 1994, when co-author Lorelei Kelly spent a semester working in the House of Representatives for Congresswoman Elizabeth Furse (D-OR). Representative Furse, a member of the Armed Services Committee, was interested in helping shift the priorities in the security policy debate toward prevention and peacekeeping. Her hope was that the conflict resolution movement across the United States would provide compelling information to spur the political will to change priorities.

The following insights gathered from a wide range of opinion leaders during interviews conducted in 1994 capture the opportunities and problems that *SNC* was created to address:

> "This is the gold rush stage of the conflict resolution movement—it is full of chaos and excitement and claims— sort of like a mining camp. Well, now we need to find some city planners." (*Head of a nonprofit*)

> "We don't need any more seminars in the Capitol conference rooms. What we need is to be told by a significant number of constituents that this idea is a good one, and that they will support our risk-taking policy initiatives. And these folks who support us need to be talking from a common and coherent script. It needs to be reliable." (*Member of Congress*)

"There is no resistance to these ideas in the US Government, and in fact, there is substantial lip-service; there are budget limitations, however. The agencies want to do their existing programs well. Remember, this bureaucracy was not set up to do this; it was hired to fight the Cold War. Before they'll change, they need 'yes-able' propositions." (*Former Department of Defense official*)

"What we in the activist world may do is increase the evidence, make the possibility real, and then help translate it into the reality of operating in Washington." (*Staff member of an international humanitarian nonprofit*)

"The conflict resolution movement is not an anti-Pentagon movement. In fact, the Pentagon promotes and has succeeded in providing some of the best examples of conflict resolution policy that exist within an agency." (*Scholar at the federally funded United States Institute of Peace*)

"One mistake would be the chip-on-the-shoulder, moralizing type of attitude, like movements of the past." (*Local activist*)

"One thing that interested academic constituencies could do is to take some issue that DC is concerned about (like democracy policy) and use the Washington jargon to hook people in and then expose them to all this other thinking." (*Think-tank scholar*)

The comments and information generated from myriad interviews and discussions led to a basic research question: how could we leverage the knowledge of academics and on-the-ground experts—local, federal, and international—in a manner helpful to policymakers? What could be done to bridge the disconnect between and within the existing, anachronistic federal bureaucracies? How could conflict resolution itself be applied to an inherently divisive institution such as Congress?

THEORY INTO PRACTICE

Conflict Resolution Principles and *Security for a New Century*

Security for a New Century is a case study in moving from conflict resolution theory to practice. For more than two decades, California's Hewlett Foundation supported organizations working to anticipate and respond to domestic and international conflict; prevent and resolve disputes; facilitate systemic change in states; and promote deliberation and participation in democratic decision-making. With these goals in mind, several universities across the United States were funded to set up conflict resolution theory-building projects and create a solid repository of knowledge in this new field.[3] At Stanford, this movement gave rise to the Stanford Center on Conflict and Negotiation (SCCN). The framework and ground rules of *Security for a New Century* are based on the theories produced at SCCN.

The Stanford Center on Conflict and Negotiation was established to explore structural, strategic, and psychological barriers that prevent parties—whether individuals, groups, or nations—from reaching mutually advantageous agreements, and also to study policies and interventions that might overcome those barriers. Research began with a few central questions: why do negotiations so often fail even when there are possible resolutions that would obviously serve disputants better than protracted struggle? Also, if resolutions are achieved, why does success often come after heavy and avoidable costs? These questions spurred discussion on business and legal disputes, and encouraged researchers to explore the numerous religious, ethnic, and political conflicts that impose staggering costs on the world.[4]

Research on conflict and negotiation lends itself to interdisciplinary exploration because crosscutting themes like decision-making and participation do not belong to any one area of

---

[3] For more information about these programs, see the "field infrastructure" section of the William and Flora Hewlett Foundation's website at www.hewlett.org.

[4] Kenneth Arrow, Robert H. Mnookin, Lee Ross, Amos Tversky, and Robert Wilson, eds., *Barriers to Conflict Resolution* (New York: W.W. Norton and Company, 1995), p. 5.

academic inquiry. Important components of *Security for a New Century* were derived from the knowledge gained from many schools of research, including social psychology, law, business, and economics, to name a few. The study group focused on highly charged political environments, interpersonal communication obstacles, and interpersonal misunderstandings, each of which have significant implications for policymaking. Conflict resolution theory—like many products of academia—can be dense and even overwhelming. But thankfully, it can be broken down into basic concepts that seem much more practical. The creators of the study group set out to distill user-friendly adaptations from esoteric concepts and then use the resulting insights as the foundation of the study group itself. What follows is a list of the most important guiding concepts modified for the study group:

Naïve Realism.

This is a general term to describe how some individuals relate in society and to the world they perceive around them. For example, if I am a naïve realist, I think that my own view of the world is objective and realistic, and therefore shared. If I share my information with others, I believe that they will endorse my point of view. If they don't, they are probably irrational or biased. A key part of naïve realism is the tendency for individuals to insist that the way they see issues is the way things really are.

False Consensus Effect.

This effect is a corollary to naïve realism—it arises because individuals tend to overestimate the extent to which others share their views. Thus they make insufficient allowance for differences in how others frame or construe information. The unfortunate result of this over-estimation of common ground is misunderstanding and unwarranted inferences about others' values, beliefs, and even sincerity. False consensus is exacerbated to the degree that individuals tend only to associate with and talk to others who share their views.

False Polarization.

This concept describes the seeming opposite, but actually complementary, notion to false consensus. It describes the underestimation of common ground that occurs when individuals consider the position of those on the "other side." Here the problem is that once we know someone disagrees with us, we think his views must reflect his own self-interest or ideology (e.g., "If he were truly objective, there would be no disagreement.") False polarization also occurs because decisiveness resonates with an audience more than ambivalence. For various strategic, social, and political reasons, many of us are generally unwilling to acknowledge our own ambivalence or uncertainty publicly, and consequently find it difficult to appreciate valid arguments on the other side.

Fundamental Attribution Error.

This term describes how individuals often fail to understand other perspectives when they encounter surprising, unexpected, or perhaps even unwarranted, responses from someone who holds those views. They tend to attribute any action or outcome to the person's disposition (or character) and fail to factor in situational circumstances. This is particularly relevant in the social or political realm. In other words, someone making a fundamental attribution error might judge a response by concluding, "I knew it, he's a liberal/conservative," instead of acknowledging the complexity of the issue at hand by reflecting, "yes, this situation is confusing," or "I'll bet his experience makes what I'm saying seem strange."

Labeling.

This concept relates to the tendency of individuals to use shorthand to overestimate differences and underestimate common ground, leading them to miss important common values in the process. This tendency manifests as stereotyping where one word substitutes for a complex and layered explanation. The best example of this in Congress is when Members use the shorthand provided by the party leadership, i.e., a bumpersticker formulation, to express their positions, instead of seeing the issue as a problem-solving opportunity. A label is used instead of breaking the issue down to more complex, but also more meaningful, parts.

Framing.

This is a counterpart to labeling and refers to whatever manipulation or technique one uses to change the way a decision or problem is understood. Simply put, framing describes an issue's terms of reference—or how a question is approached. How is a problem formulated? An example of framing is the question: Is the glass half-full or half-empty? The description of the question (the glass in this case) can significantly influence the listener's response and/or choice of next steps. Framing for maximum polarization is common with controversial political issues—where the language used to introduce the issue gives away a bias. Defense issues are often framed as either/or budget trade-offs, with rhetoric about who is "strong" or "weak" on defense. Each of these frames denotes a particular interpretation of the issue and leaves out many important details and complexities. In political debates, issues are often framed in absolute terms, and partisans use misinterpretations or even purposefully put the wrong construction on the words or actions of their perceived opponents. How an issue is framed will go far in determining the capacity for finding common ground. If there are limited opportunities to explore and resolve these tensions, conflict emerges due to the gap between real and perceived differences.

Reactive Devaluation.

This term describes a situation in which the very act of offering information or a proposal—if it comes from a supposed adversary—may diminish its value. Reactive devaluation is often seen in policymaking as a partisan cue, making a situation so toxic that sharing and problem solving become impossible.

Loss Aversion.

For individuals, this concept entails a reluctance to accept risks unless the payoffs are very favorable. It describes an individual's tendency to avoid immediate loss, even if the apparent cost is more than offset by a future gain. Loss aversion favors the status quo. The term also refers to the asymmetry in the evaluation of positive and negative outcomes, as losses loom larger than the corresponding gains. It points to the superiority of certainty (that which I have now) over mere probability (that which I might have in the future).

Information Asymmetry.

This concept is often found in discussions of financial markets, where some, but not all participants know information. For our purposes, it is used to describe information about peace and security issues as a public good—one that is distributed unequally because of systematic informational and political barriers inherent to Congress. Conflict prevention improves to the extent that information asymmetry is reduced. While recognizing that good faith can't be assumed in politics, the study group addressed this question: how do we optimize information sharing to prevent these issues from falling victim to partisan politics?

The preceding terms outlined important considerations for the founders of *Security for a New Century*. The perceptions and actions of politicians on Capitol Hill provide an ideal laboratory for observing each of these concepts at work on a daily basis. Given the conditions of naïve realism, attribution errors, loss aversion, and unevenly distributed information, how might we engage problem solving in an environment that is both focused on the short term, and often antagonistic? Moreover, how might we do this during times of transition and uncertainty like after the Cold War, and then following September 11th?

Applying the Principles

From its inception, the study group reflected conflict resolution research, taking advantage of solid empirical knowledge in the art and science of peace-making and participatory systems. The study group was a test case of conflict resolution theory. The founders were interested in how individuals use information to make decisions, and what kind of information is most desirable in the process. The stakes were high: Congress is a contentious battleground of ideas where framing issues is a competitive sport. The fast-changing agenda makes uncertainty an important consideration, while the egos and political implications of public positions render elected leaders risk-averse. Moreover, our target audience was Hill staffers who are wary of information shared by outsiders, especially lobbyists and those seeking to have a biased perspective. Let us turn to how the art and science of conflict resolution was applied in our approach to creating and implementing *Security for a New Century*.

The study group was founded on the premise that the major impediment to congressional support for US cooperative engagement is information asymmetry. In other words, that many Members were defaulting to Cold War thinking or just taking cues from party leadership because credible alternatives were not available. As we've discussed already, the deliberative process of Congress is hindered by dated concepts, distorted by narrow jurisdictions, and lacking in feedback mechanisms for problem-solving. The lack of unbiased, timely, and authoritative information seemed like a challenge we could address. As one of the founding goals of the study group was to create a feedback loop between Congress and US policy agencies, we actively searched for active or recently retired government policy professionals who could share a "ground truth" perspective. Viewed this way, the study group also amplified the ability of Congress to conduct thorough oversight.

Examples of reactive devaluation occur often in Washington's policy debates. Partisan politics required us to prevent the automatic discounting of speakers because of a suspicion of bias by being particularly careful about who addressed the study group. Hence, we avoided "big names" and/or individuals with an obvious party affiliation. To this day, our ideal speaker is an individual who understands the broad nature of security and the interagency aspects of policy, but who also had much practical experience implementing policy. This tactic also helps avoid the perception that the speakers come with a particular agenda. In order to maximize the learning experience, we treat participants as potential naïve realists, with the corresponding understanding that we need to prevent attribution errors as much as possible. Providing for naïve realism has been relatively simple. Peace and security issues allow much room for identifying common values. How these values are prioritized with funding resources, however, is often where conflicts arise, especially if the issues are framed as trade-offs or policy opposites, (i.e., "guns versus butter") instead of policy alternatives.

Peace and security issues also suffer because of a hangover of bitter political legacies from decades past, as discussed in Chapter 2. For this reason, it was imperative at the outset not to allow our topics and speakers to be categorically dismissed through easy stereotypes ("He's a jarhead, what does he know about peace-building?" or "Why should I come listen to the Birkenstock crowd talk about security?") Hence, our charge is to find "unusual suspects" to discuss issues. We have done this by inviting military professionals to address the humanitarian or soft aspects of security needs in which they actively have played a role, such as AIDS and disaster relief. We also invite economic development and relief specialists to discuss how their issues are part of post-Cold War security, and how they often work in partnership with the military to achieve overall goals. Mixing and matching in this way does not come without tension and debate, but it is where the power of the study group framework comes in handy. Ground rules have been established. Everyone present knows that the purpose is dialogue and information sharing, not political point scoring. These values have been our reference points. The fact that neither the framework nor the ground rules have changed during the life of the study group is a testament to the power of careful framing.

Attribution errors occur when individuals don't sufficiently account for perspectives different from their own. We assume that if individuals come to the study group, they come with an open mind, and that our purpose is to offer as much solid knowledge and creative problem-solving as possible. Our task is to prevent, to the extent possible, the tendency for staff to close their minds about creative, pragmatic alternatives.

Conflict resolution theory highlights the important role of an objective third party to act as mediator or facilitator. The study group designates the host as facilitator. The "host" is a staffer, not an outsider. In a partisan "winner-takes-all" place like Capitol Hill, the facilitator's objective is to foster a problem-solving atmosphere and encourage discussion, thereby creating an opportunity for participants to think in new ways about a particular security challenge.

> "In a sense, the mediator can turn the parties' attention away from the direct pursuit of equity to the pursuit of enlightened self-interest. While divergent views of the past are inevitable, the mediator can employ techniques designed to at least help each side understand the case from the other side's perspective."[5]

---

[5] Kenneth Arrow et al., eds., *Barriers to Conflict Resolution*, p. 22.

The active facilitation of a third party is essential. From the outset, it has been vital to give the content center stage, underscoring the basic framework of security as a broadly shared concern that has complex parts. It also stresses that this understanding of security requires many policy tools. In practice, this means no long-winded introductions or announcements. Rather, the facilitator blends in with the rest of the audience after a brief introduction, then reappears to help with questions and answers. The invited guests are also issued advance "Speaker Guidelines" with tips on how to prepare for and connect with a congressional audience. Occasionally, the facilitator intervenes to clarify, repeat questions, redirect interrogative questioning, and clear up obvious misunderstandings.

Finally, it has been important to construct the study group in a way that minimizes the effects of loss aversion. This has been especially important after September 11th. Although September 11th made broad notions of security more obvious, it also revealed the inertia of the policy conversations of the post-Cold War 1990s, when many opportunities for dramatically reframing security were marginalized or ignored. September 11th, therefore, encouraged lawmakers to begin questioning both narrowly defined security issues and the reliance on traditional methods of providing for security through higher defense spending. Like the American people, many lawmakers' initial reactions to September 11th were anger and fear. Through the study group, governmental agencies, congressional staff, and the policy community engaged in discussion about a more comprehensive vision of peace and long-term security. The study group attracts superb participants, and only rarely suffers from the antics of disruptive attendees. To illustrate, here are just a few topics the study group has covered:

Hearts and Minds: An Arab Reformist's Perspective
With Dr. Hossam Badrawi, Chairman of the Education and Scientific Research Committee in the Egyptian Parliament and leader within the reformist wing of the National Democratic Party.

The Iraq Survey Group

With Dr. David Kay, former Special Advisor to the Iraq Survey Group and Chief US Weapons Inspector in Iraq.

The US Role in UN Peacekeeping

With Dr. Jane Holl Lute, Assistant Secretary-General, UN Department of Peacekeeping Operations.

The US Army: Transforming to What?

With Colonel Douglas A. MacGregor, Center for Technology and National Security Policy, National Defense University.

Techniques and Tactics in Practice

The actual practice of the study group encompasses conflict resolution techniques such as facilitated dialogue, not-for-attribution discussion, a problem-solving framework, and "ground truth" perspectives of operational experts (policy implementers) as frequently as possible. For Hill staff who are often jaded by constant advocacy and lobbyists plugging commercial interests, the study group was a welcome respite and an instant hit.

Security for a New Century was created as a flexible venue to respond to the needs of Hill staff on issues where background knowledge can inform current policymaking (e.g., lessons learned in the Haiti peacekeeping mission during the 1990s and how those lessons might apply to our policies in Iraq). We also decided to open most of the meetings to off-the-Hill participants in order to demystify Congress for those working on peace and security issues in and around Washington, DC. Most importantly, however, the principle of inclusion has been foremost, so all participants can hear as many perspectives as possible on the issue being discussed.

The purpose of *Security for a New Century* is simple: to broaden the international outlook on Capitol Hill in the interest of the public good. The overarching premise, endowing the study group with a problem-solving (not political) ethic, is that the Cold War is over and that we need a better understanding of contemporary threats and solutions. Moreover, we want to reap the good intentions of elected leaders who generally agree that when it comes to US security, military force should be used only as an option of last resort. If our guiding principles are indeed true, then we have many areas to explore—areas that carry with them significant policy implications.

Framing an Updated Worldview

Security for a New Century set out not only to frame the security challenges of globalization consistently, but also to root this notion of change in reality by using specific examples. We needed a basic framework within which participants would be asked to construe global peace and security issues. We therefore decided early on to map the discussions of the study group according to the proposition that today's security issues: (1) exist *across* as much as *within* traditional boundaries; (2) are *affected* by constantly evolving communications technology; and, (3) require new and nontraditional partnerships, both public and private.

One way we hope to foster participation in the study group has been to highlight the opportunity for fairness in discussion. In comparison to committee hearings, which are Member-focused, formal, and stage-managed, the study group recognizes no formal hierarchy. The only exception to this rule has been that Hill staff are recognized first during the question and answer period. It is our hope that if discussants feel heard, the knowledge gained will have more legitimacy. Other ground rules have also been established: the study group is off-the-record and breaks on the hour; its guests avoid acronyms; and it is not an advocacy venue.

For the study group to be perceived and function as a shared resource and a public service, we decided that its activities must be transparent and inclusive. The first step in this undertaking was to make sure the project had bipartisan sponsorship.

The second important task has been to make sure that all staff are invited every time. This has been accomplished via the use of internal mail. The study group's "Dear Colleague" letters are signed by the co-sponsoring Members and alert staff to upcoming events. A typical *SNC* "Dear Colleague" might read as follows:

Dear Colleague:

Security for a New Century 108th Congress

Toons Routing Out Terror

When: Monday, March 25 at 3:00 pm
Where: Hart Senate Office Building, Room 454

Roger Rabbit, former movie star turned CIA supersleuth, will be on hand to discuss the operations of toons in investigating terrorist financing networks, efforts to track their origins, and techniques utilized to identify persons involved in them. Special Agent Rabbit will discuss the flexibility inherent in an organization that is charged with the investigation of a covert structure that utilizes everything from gold to diamonds as its means to move money among many countries and continents. The questions he will address include: What have we learned about terrorist financing networks since September 11th? What types of international cooperation are required to help facilitate US investigative efforts? In what aspects are these efforts lacking?

Security for a New Century is a bipartisan study group for Congress. We meet regularly with US and international policy professionals to discuss the post-Cold War and post-September 11th security environment. All sessions are facilitated and off-the-record. It is not an advocacy venue.

Sincerely,

Senator So-and-So (R)   Senator So-and-So (D)

"Dear Colleagues" are supplemented by internal email notices to alert staff about sessions. The email list for Hill staff is all-inclusive, so all staffers are notified each time. Off-the-Hill lists are compiled via self-referral and sign-up sheets.

It continues to be the main goal of *Security for a New Century* to highlight forward-thinking efforts and to seek the silver lining of the difficult lessons learned from September 11th. By raising the general level of knowledge about international issues on Capitol Hill, and by stressing the importance of American leadership in forging international cooperation, the study group has provided a practical example of conflict resolution theory in action. By showcasing authoritative knowledge and organizing a forum for dialogue, it has bolstered issues of common concern, made complex issues apprehensible, and positively reframed many policy alternatives as a choice between the better of two goods rather than the lesser of two evils.

Security for a New Century is a balanced voice that highlights the benefits of active cooperation on peace and security issues. It is just one of many possible ways to help elected leaders move past the institutional barriers that keep Congress stuck in old-fashioned or partisan ways of thinking. We look forward to seeing similar endeavors as you and your colleagues organize to pursue the same goal.

Conclusion

What constitutes security in the post-Cold War and post-September 11th world? What tools are necessary to address today's threats? How can the US harness its awesome power and global position to achieve and sustain "peace and security"?

We are convinced that security must be broadly defined in order to address the complex, diffuse, and interrelated challenges we face. In light of this fact, the tools needed will necessarily run the gamut, from sophisticated weapons and a well-trained military to "fight and win the nation's wars," to well-honed diplomatic, economic, and political instruments to address the numerous challenges that cannot be addressed through the use of force. This is not a partisan issue. Ensuring that our elected leaders are protecting and promoting the common good is, in fact, our patriotic duty.

If we agree on the need for a well-stocked toolkit to achieve peace and security, then much work remains to bring about the necessary changes in perceptions and priorities. The structural imbalances and institutional barriers to bring about change may appear quite daunting. We must overcome anachronistic Cold War perceptions that bigger defense budgets are necessarily the equivalent of more security. We also must be willing to question whether the allocations in any defense budget hit the right balance between the acquisition of hardware and the human resources upon which our security ultimately depends. This balance between hardware and human capital applies to national security investments well beyond the Pentagon.

What is required is a nuts-and-bolts strategy that can help challenge prevalent but potentially anachronistic assumptions, level the playing field between peddlers of hardware and promoters of preventive measures, and leverage parochialism to demonstrate a constituency for US cooperative security. Only with a solid strategy and sufficient momentum to implement that strategy will we begin to chip away at any one of these challenges and manage to meet our ultimate objective: creating the political will to make "peace and security" a priority through an investment strategy appropriate to today's international challenges.

The US Congress, despite its institutional shortcomings, offers possibilities for creative problem-solving that are unique within the federal government. 535 individual elected leaders work on Capitol Hill, each with the potential to engage in new ways of setting priorities and governing. More importantly, Congress offers the most diverse set of possibilities for individual citizens to effect change. At the same time, given the vast menu of entry points, the time constraints, and the need to overcome some firmly entrenched institutional barriers, a focused strategy is important.

It is our hope that this manual provides you with the minimum tools and resources you need to devise your own strategy and leverage the possibilities available on Capitol Hill. The momentum behind implementation of this strategy rests on the willingness of people like you, who believe your voice should be part of the chorus urging positive change for a peaceful and prosperous global future.

Appendix:
A Final Word on Outreach

ADVOCACY, LOBBYING, AND EDUCATION

In the world of nonprofits, federal employees, think tanks, and philanthrophy, a common "scary story" sounds something like this: NGO employee X was seen talking to Hill staff at a public meeting. Several days later, he was accused of lobbying, and his name was broadcast all over the Internet. He had to abandon his career and leave town, and now lives on a tiny island off the coast of Greenland.

Such legends understandably cause even knowledgeable individuals to err on the side of caution in offering their expertise, avoiding Congress altogether. This is especially true for philanthropically funded individuals who talk to Members of Congress in a professional capacity (as a university professor, for instance). Why, they reason, take a chance trying to inform Congress if it might lead to trouble?

The fear and confusion about lobbying exacerbates the public feedback imbalance on peace and security issues in Congress. After all, a host of important voices—specialists and practitioners in their fields—are often missing from congressional discussions on foreign and defense policy. As a result, the potential for achieving a well-stocked policy toolkit is diminished. In addition, federal employees are not allowed to contact Congress on behalf of their programs, except under narrow circumstances.[1] These limitations on communications between agencies and Capitol Hill make one of cooperative security's best information assets difficult to exploit.

Sometimes foreign policy experts and concerned citizens try to inform their legislators in indirect ways, such as a book sent to Capitol Hill or emails linking to scholarly journal articles. The authors then get discouraged when nothing happens—no follow-up, not even a "thanks."

---

[1] See 18 U.S.C. 1913.

KNOWING THE BASICS

Academic specialists and "on the ground" practitioners must achieve a higher profile in Congress before a full spectrum of peace and security issues becomes a priority in its deliberations. These same individuals—peace and security "knowledge brokers"—must be involved in discussing problems and issues and laying out a framework for understanding today's wide ranging security concerns. Such activity *in no way* constitutes lobbying. We hope to encourage our readers to feel confident in presenting quality factual information, so that their elected leaders and others can make well-informed, independent decisions about security issues. This should be welcome news to those who just want to provide new research findings, communicate the success of their international project, or help Members think more broadly about alternatives. This is education, pure and simple.

It is also important to recognize the difference between lobbying and advocacy. Most policy advocacy is not lobbying, so it does not pose a threat to an organization's tax exemption. Although most people use the words interchangeably, there is a distinction between advocacy and lobbying that is helpful to understand. When nonprofit organizations advocate on their own behalf, they seek to affect some aspect of society, whether they appeal to individuals about their behavior, employers about their rules, or the government about its laws. Advocacy, therefore, is directed at *improving* common-good big picture issues with the assumption being that there is a charitable public service aspect involved. Lobbying, on the other hand, refers to advocacy efforts that directly attempt to influence specific legislation. This distinction is helpful to keep in mind because it means that laws limiting the lobbying done by nonprofit organizations do not govern other advocacy activities.[2]

Political activities and legislative activities are two different things, and are subject to two different sets of rules. The parameters for political discussion are more generous than our scary story would suggest.[3]

---

[2] An Advocacy/Lobbying toolkit is available online from the Connecticut Nonprofit Information Network at www.ctnonprofits.org

[3] See "Political and Lobbying Activities"; Internal Revenue Service; available online at http://www.irs.gov/charities/charitable/article/0,,id=120703,00.html.

Consider the following examples, which do NOT constitute lobbying:

- Providing nonpartisan analysis or research that presents all sides of a policy issue;

- Examining and discussing broad social, economic, and political problems;

- Conveying your technical expertise and opinion on a substantive issue in response to a written request from a Member;

- Making recommendations, (even offering opinions) about different policy options;

- Telling your Member of Congress about the new peace studies department—its functions, missions, and successes—at a local public university event to which she was invited;

- Asking your Member of Congress to participate in a home-town event, such as "A Discussion with Local Heroes: Peacekeeping in the Balkans";

- Presenting your Member of Congress with a list of signatures that supports a well-known international initiative on Israeli-Palestinian reconciliation;

- Telling your Member of Congress that you know about and appreciate the government agencies responsible for conflict prevention and peacebuilding.

Again, lobbying consists of communications that are intended to influence specific legislation. Consider the following example: An appointment with a defense staffer to demonstrate your "gravity-defying peace and tranquility capsule" and ask for more research and development funding in the defense appropriations bill *would* constitute lobbying, because this activity explicitly refers to funding in an existing bill. Conversely, asking your Member to help organize a staff briefing to discuss your peace studies department's recent conference findings on good governance in conflict-prone societies would not.

Lobbying for Nonprofits

Whether or not one intends to discuss legislation, it is important to understand the Internal Revenue Service's (IRS) rules for lobbying. In 1976, recognizing the need to help constituencies that have a limited voice in the policy process, the IRS acted to remedy the confusion about lobbying by making it easier for small and average-sized public charities to add their voices to the process without fear of jeopardizing their nonprofit status.

If you intend to influence specific legislation, it is usually in your best interests to send in what the IRS calls the 501 (h) election, using Form 5768. It is one of the two ways you can measure your lobbying limits, and it allows for greater capacity and guidance than the alternate measurement system, known as the "insubstantial part" test.[4]

The tax code allows for much more latitude in what constitutes "lobbying" than most people ever seek to exploit. In addition, many educational opportunities exist that fall far short of lobbying and are never exercised. Only when nonprofits and educators working for the public good take full advantage of the opportunity to add their voices to the peace and security policy discussion will we see a more level playing field on Capitol Hill.

---

[4] See, in particular, "Worry-Free Lobbying for Nonprofits"; Alliance for Justice; available online at http://www.allianceforjustice.org/images/collection_images/ Worry-Free%20Lobbying.pdf. Further information is available at www.clpi.org, maintained by Charity Lobbying in the Public Interest.

About the Authors

Lorelei Kelly is a Senior Associate and Co-Director for the *Security for a New Century* project, a bipartisan study group that she founded in 1998 while on the staff of Congresswoman Elizabeth Furse (D-OR) and that is now based at the Henry L. Stimson Center. She came to Washington in 1997 from Stanford University's Center on Conflict and Negotiation. Her professional interest in international affairs and conflict resolution began in 1989 when she witnessed the end of the Cold War as a Watson Fellow living in Berlin. She was later trained as a mediator and worked at the Oregon Peace Institute. Her background in organizing provided the impetus for *Security for a New Century*.

Elizabeth Turpen is a Senior Associate and Co-Director for the *Security for a New Century* project. She brings recent Senate experience and a background in national security, nuclear, and nonproliferation issues. Dr. Turpen's previous employment was with Senator Pete V. Domenici (R-NM) as a Legislative Assistant responsible for defense, nonproliferation, and foreign affairs. Prior to coming to Washington in 1998, she was a consultant on nonproliferation policy, US-Russia programs, and the national security implications of technological advances for a high-tech company in New Mexico. Dr. Turpen has extensive teaching experience and has published numerous articles. She received her Ph.D. from the Fletcher School of Law and Diplomacy at Tufts University.